SHAPLAND & PETTER Ltd.

OF BARNSTAPLE.

Arts & Crafts Furniture

Daryl Bennett

First published by Museum of Barnstaple and North Devon 2005

The moral right of the author has been asserted.

Copyright © Museum of Barnstaple and North Devon and Daryl Bennett

Cover Design Paul Gilby and Daryl Bennett

ISBN No. 0 9550316 0 5

Designed and Printed by Ruddocks Print, Lincoln, England

Front Cover and this page: Mahogany bureau with hand-beaten copper panel and inscription. R1529
Frontispiece: Repoussé copper panel with applied and inset enamel
Left: Door of mahogany cabinet with inlaid design

Foreword

This book is one of the products of the Heritage Lottery Funded project "Shapland and Petter of Barnstaple: 150 years". Based on the Shapland and Petter collection at the Museum of Barnstaple & North Devon, the project owes its existence to both the single-minded enthusiasm of Daryl Bennett, and to the depth of local feeling within Barnstaple for the town's largest employer of the 20th century.

Between 1996 and 1999 the successor company, then known as NT Shapland and Petter, passed some pieces of Arts and Crafts furniture and a large photographic archive into the care of the Museum of Barnstaple and North Devon. Over subsequent years the display at the museum, supplemented by additional pieces bought at auction, attracted the attention of furniture collectors, leading to continuous use of the archive. We came to the realisation that the firm was of more than local importance.

In 2002, Daryl Bennett approached the museum with an idea for an exhibition and book. The project which emerged also encompassed digitisation of the company archive, a celebratory 150 year booklet by Margaret Reed and an oral history project. Along the way the team, including over 30 volunteers, has explored archives across the country, located and acquired important catalogues, digitised thousands of photographs and interviewed many past and present workers at the firm.

We hope this book will serve as a lasting and useful record of the project. It demonstrates to furniture collectors the range and quality of furniture made in this distant corner of Devon. And we hope Barnstaple people will appreciate how important the company's products have been and the important part they played in the dissemination of Arts and Crafts style around the world.

Alison Mills, Museum of Barnstaple and North Devon

Acknowledgments

The creation of this book has been a part of a larger programme of work funded by the Heritage Lottery Fund and supported by the Museum of Barnstaple and North Devon, Leaderflush Shapland, the Friends of the Museum and the Barnstaple Bridge Trust. From the beginning, the professional advice, leadership and practical help of Alison Mills at the museum has been a crucial factor in the success of the work. In the early days of planning and securing funding, Helen Wheatley at the Heritage Lottery Fund provided the technical help and enthusiasm which gave us the confidence to establish the proposal and during the project, Kelly Spry-Phare guided our progress.

The Steering group, formed in Barnstaple has taken on the task of directing the project, ably and enthusiastically coordinated by Claire Gulliver. Sue Lane and Mark Stevens of Leaderflush Shapland, Sarah Montague from the Park School, and Mary Cameron, have all played important roles in carrying out parts of the work.

Significant help has been received in researching and compiling the evidence from the National Art Library at the Victoria and Albert Museum, the Sheffield Hallam University Learning Centre, the Westminster Archives, the West Yorkshire Archive Service at Bradford, the Library, the Museum and the Athenaeum at Barnstaple. Thanks are due to Christies, Bonhams, Sotheby's and Lyon and Turnbull for allowing access to their archives and the help of Dan Tolson and Nick Burns was very much appreciated. Thanks are also due to Roxanne Peters of V&A Images for her help and professional input.

In building the knowledge base and in the acquisition of documents for the Museum I am indebted to Vance Whittall and Mark Golding. The tracking and acquisition of important examples of furniture pictured in the following pages has been greatly assisted by decorative art specialists Mark Hilton, Adam Brawn- Meek, Vincent Duffy, Matt and Liam from Art Furniture and Hillhouse Antiques. The examples of furniture shown include those kindly made available by TB and R Jordan, John Walton, Susan and Jason Hare, and Cannon Hall Museum among others.

Expert advice in the formative stages of the project from Frances Collard was much appreciated and throughout the work the encouragement and hands on help from Mary Greensted, who gave her time so generously were fundamental in helping us all to make progress and to create this book. Margaret Reed has contributed powerfully to the research, drafting and preparation of this work and has been a constant source of encouragement.

Expert advice is acknowledged from Dr Roger Shuff on religious elements and design registration, Professor Arthur Willis, on plant sciences, Mr Phillip Jameson and Dr Clive Edwards on the history of furniture construction. Special thanks are due to Mr Philip Bowditch for his help in the creating the concept for this book and his expert knowledge and practical help upon which I have drawn throughout the project.

I am particularly grateful to the staff and volunteers at the Museum of Barnstaple and North Devon, including collections manager Ruth Spires, IT expert Julian Vayne, project assistant Claire Chope and the volunteers listed below who have contributed their labour to the project. My thanks also to Dr David Pickles, Jayne Muir, Anne Mills, John Pedder and Mike Newton who supported me in work required to produce this book. Project volunteers in Barnstaple have included Gill Bradshaw, Daphne Dallyn, Ann Patrick, Katie Russell, Geraldine Sainsbury, Richard Smith, Freda Hooper, Pete Tibble, John Gulliver, Mike Welsh, Keith Davis, Sue Bromley, Nic Hoof, Moyra Keatings, Doreen Sandell, Eva Astiz, Lesley Dalladay, Brian Barrow, Anne Denyer, Justin Milford, Hayley Piper, Neville Stanikk, Pam Burgess, Doreen Sandell and Elize Bouchet.

And finally, I'd like to acknowledge the important contribution made to this book by Paul Gilby who worked hard to produce the colour photographs that have captured a stunning range of Shapland and Petter furniture, showing it at its very best.

Daryl Bennett

Introduction

This book provides a description and a celebration of the Arts and Crafts furniture made in Barnstaple by the Shapland and Petter company. It covers a period of roughly twenty years from 1894 up until 1914 and brings together the evidence base from libraries and archives, creating the starting point for a much more informed appreciation of the work of the company.

Shapland and Petter created some of the finest examples of Arts and Crafts furniture for the period and some typical and exceptional pieces are illustrated in the following pages. From the pieces shown, and those referenced in archive material it becomes possible to appreciate the creative and 'artistic' skills of the company, and to build up an understanding of the incredibly wide range of their work

A key factor in understanding and appreciating the work of the company has been the development of the evidence base in the form of documents and photographs from the period which enable positive and definite attribution of pieces. In the past, attribution has tended to be based on commercial needs rather than any scientific principles and many of the best examples of Shapland and Petter furniture have not been recognised or have been attributed to other companies. In developing the evidence base, the intention is to help re-assign the credit for these fine pieces and to affirm the very significant contribution of Shapland and Petter to the Arts and Crafts style.

The consideration of the evidence base started with the archive of photographs and company documents which were given by the company (now Leaderflush Shapland) to the Museum of Barnstaple and North Devon. Further research in the National Art Library, other archives and auction houses provided evidence from period journals, trade literature and pictures of known pieces. Further progress was made via contact through the author's website when an original and comprehensive catalogue High Class Furniture was discovered and subsequently acquired for the Museum in 2004. Another important document, referred to as the Catalogue of Drawings was discovered in 2005 and offered to the Museum. These different elements make up the evidence base from which it becomes possible to identify key characteristic of design construction and decoration.

The information now available on Shapland and Petter provides a stimulus to review some commonplace assumptions about the Arts and Crafts style, and the linked notions of Liberty style or British Art Nouveau. There has perhaps been a tendency to group together and merge similar styles without much rigour in attribution. There also seems to have been a strong focus on London in the establishment of the Arts and Crafts movement and its commercial development. The research and local history presented here, centred on Barnstaple is intended to increase the understanding of how the movement developed outside of London, adding to the knowledge we have already about the Cotswolds, Birmingham, Keswick, Newlyn and other parts of the country.

As the London focus has drawn interest away from provincial companies another influence, which could be referred to as 'the great man theory of history,' has concentrated attention on leading designers and entrepreneurs, and encouraged us to ignore the less famous. However, to understand the development of the Shapland and Petter style, it is important to look behind the celebrities and consider the cultural factors and social impulses which created a market for their work. One observation here is that Arts and Crafts style became a fashion, at the turn of the century and even from Barnstaple, Shapland and Petter were right at the heart of the supply network for London and other major cities in Britain. It is clear that designers at Shapland and Petter could appreciate and work within the fashion for the 'artistic' and were able to add their own creative interpretation to great effect..

In considering the contribution of Shapland and Petter to Arts and Crafts style some interesting paradoxes have been highlighted. Their use of machinery, advertising and their marketing strategies may seem to contradict Arts and Crafts principles. Their image as providers of modern and fashionable furniture does not seem to fit in with a movement which looked back to mediaeval times, rejecting industrial progress. In appreciating their social value however, the overriding factor is that the company thrived, their economic success enabling a large workforce to develop their crafts and skills, and earn a wage to support their families. So, whilst not a Utopian social experiment, the enterprise of Shapland and Petter generated enormous cultural and social benefit for the working people of Barnstaple. The furniture which they created, as well as being useful, beautiful and a joy to live with represents a most significant part of our cultural heritage.

Excellence of Finish, Combined with Economy **in Price.**

SHAPLAND & PETTER · L^{TD}
RALEIGH · WORKS · BARNSTAPLE

HIGH CLASS
FURNITURE
& FITMENTS
OF ORIGINAL
CHARACTER

LONDON SHOW
ROOMS
61 BERNERS S^T
OXFORD S^T W

Goods suitable for
Christmas Presents
on view at 61, Berners Street, W.

Send for Booklet of Illustrations if you cannot
call.

1.1 Shapland and Petter Advertisement. Furniture Record. Nov 1905

Chapter One Artistic Furniture

In this chapter the development of the Arts and Crafts movement will be introduced briefly and the social factors which helped to create the market for Arts and Crafts furniture will be considered.

Shapland and Petter produced a wide range of furniture in the Arts and Crafts style designed to appeal to the growing market of middle class consumers who wanted tasteful homes and modern, artistic furniture. In the mid 1890s the design and decoration of their furniture followed the progressive designers such as M.H. Baillie Scott and C.F.A. Voysey who developed the Arts and Crafts style established by William Morris. The popularity and appeal of Arts and Crafts increased from the first Arts and Crafts Exhibition in 1888 to a broad movement publicised through artistic journals and magazines such as *The Artist* and *The Studio*, and ever growing commercial networks supplying the new consumers by the end of the nineteenth century.

The single most important factor that enabled Shapland and Petter to produce their range was that people wanted to buy it. The simple economics of supply and demand sustained the business as a whole and it is clear from their advertising material at the turn of the century that the image which they wanted to sell their work was an artistic one. Whilst they continued producing the range of period and revival styles, the artistic range must have been the most dynamic side of the business and an essential source of income and profit. In the last decade of the nineteenth century the taste for artistic furniture, which began as a ripple centred around a few shops in London, increased to a broad based preference as the new style or 'new art movement' became fashionable. Shapland and Petter caught this wave of fashion, helping to take artistic furniture to towns and cities across the country through their innovative manufacturing and marketing skills.

Early days of the Arts and Crafts movement

In explaining the background to the history of Shapland and Petter it is important to bear in mind two central themes within the mid nineteenth century. Firstly the interest in revivalism and fascination with historical models, and secondly the preoccupation with the style and techniques of ornament and decoration. Both themes are particularly relevant to Shapland and Petter as they provided the cultural context which created the demand for their furniture and the artistic traditions upon which they based many of their designs.

There is a long history to the artistic design and decoration of furniture, and the tradition of decorated furniture into which Shapland and Petter fit so well is probably best understood by starting with the Great Exhibition in London in 1851. The exhibition held at the Crystal Palace in Hyde Park, in London, featured the very latest in scientific progress and industrial design. Alongside the modern however, there was a very special part of the exhibition, A.N. Wilson observed:-

'But as we have accustomed ourselves to seeing this exhibition as the symbol of the nineteenth century industrial progress and materialism we turn the corner and - what is this? We are standing in the Medieaval Court designed by Augustus Welby Pugin. In which we are confronted with Gothic High Altars, hanging lamps and statues of the Virgin' [1]

Pugin, when he designed the Medieaval Court, was primarily an architect of churches and religious objects and was perhaps the most influential of those architects who wished to revive the Medieaval or Gothic taste. The movement which followed his lead, established a firm reaction against machines and championed the revival of craftsmanship, honesty in construction and 'truth to materials' which became the fundamental principles of the Arts and Crafts tradition. By 1858 there was growing interest in painted furniture amongst architects, artists and designers and the Architectural Exhibition in that year included painted furniture by William Morris and William Burges. An important milestone for development of the 'artistic style' was the International Exhibition of 1862 in London, which was of great importance in the history of furniture, interior decoration and the development of taste in the nineteenth century. The exhibition included a Medieaval Court which featured a painted and inlaid sideboard by William Burges and showed the first exhibits of the newly established firm of Morris, Marshall Faulkner and Company.

Morris, Marshall Faulkner and Company

The 'Firm' of Morris, Marshall and Faulkner was established in 1861. Their exhibits at the 1862 exhibition included spectacular pieces of furniture in the form of simple cupboards and cabinets with panels painted by William Morris, Burne-Jones, and other members of the Pre-Raphaelite circle. Morris himself referred to this distinction between:-

'The necessary workaday furniture... simple to the last degree and there is the other kind of what I shall call state furniture; I mean

1.2 Stained and painted glass. circa. 1862. Rossetti, Dante Gabriel, for Morris, Marshall, Faulkner & Co. V&A C.318-1927

1.3 The Yatman Cabinet. 1858. William Burges. V&A 217:1, 2-1961

sideboards cabinets and the like… we need not spare ornament on these but may make them as elegant as we can with carving or inlaying or painting: these are the blossoms of the art of furniture.'[2]

Aesthetic movement and Art Furniture

Several designers were working from the 1860s through the 70s and 80s and together helped to establish 'Art Furniture' which was readily adopted by the furniture manufacturers as a distinct branch of the trade. Designers such as William Burges were driven by a strong enthusiasm for Medieaval ideas with simple structures and elaborate decoration. The revival of Gothic forms of construction influenced the work of Burges along with J.P. Seddon, Charles Eastlake, and particularly Bruce Talbert who, as a writer and designer helped to apply Gothic architectural style to domestic furniture. Talbert's designs were seen as progressive, with decorative richness inlaid with various woods and metal, inset with enamel panels and also were of a different structural shape which was rectangular in 'rabbit hutch' style. The Pet sideboard designed by him and made by Gillows in 1871 had features which were to become typical of Arts and Crafts furniture 30 years later and particularly relevant to the style of Shapland and Petter. These were:-

- Straight lines, long strap hinges and ring handles
- Cut through work or piercing and rows of spindles
- Applied enamelled plaques and painted panels
- Revealed construction showing dovetails and tenons
- Inset decorative panels and an inscribed quotation or 'motto'

Hints on Household Taste

Charles Eastlake was one of the earliest writers who attempted to influence the middle class consumer in his *Hints on Household Taste* published in 1872.[3] Important concepts which he introduces are honesty of construction, furniture should be solid and stout, and should be fit for purpose without any deception, a good design should show at first sight its real purpose. So, the appeal of a good design should be functional as well as aesthetic and these two concepts, the useful and the beautiful are always centre stage in the Arts and Crafts style.

The philosophy and beliefs

Some key forces which gave birth to the movement were:-

- Rejection of Classical and Italianate architecture, and the revival of the Gothic Style.
- Rebellion against industrialisation and mass production of poor quality goods by machines.
- Nostalgia for the medieaval age seen as the golden age of creativity and freedom.
- Belief in a socialist or Utopian society, striving for good quality of life for all.
- Desire to view artists and craftsmen as equals.
- Determination that art should be for the people, by the people not a separate or superior privilege.

1.4 Oak buffet with copper panels. R. 2125

3

1.5 Manchester Arts and Crafts Exhibition. The Studio Vol 15 1898

Arts and Crafts Societies and Exhibitions

Between 1880 and 1890 five different societies which contributed to the development of the Arts and Crafts movement were established and these paved the way for the emergence of important individual designers such as Ashbee, Lethaby, Baillie Scott and Voysey who began to receive recognition for their work. The Arts and Crafts Exhibition Society was founded in 1888 and the title represented the first use of the term 'Arts and Crafts'. The purpose of the society was to organise exhibitions, to further the ideals and the work of a group of artists and designers which included William Morris, Edward Burne-Jones and Walter Crane who became Chairman of the Society.

Whilst the Arts and Crafts movement developed in London in its formative years, other branches developed in the provinces, Manchester, and Birmingham in particular having their own Arts and Crafts Exhibitions.

Progressive furniture

Perhaps the most important influence with respect to a developing awareness of the style, was the reporting of exhibitions with photographs of exhibits in contemporary periodicals and art journals such as *The Builder*, *The Artist* and then later in *The Studio*.

Morris and Co. and the Liberty Style

The creation of taste and the fashion for Artistic, then later Arts and Crafts furniture was lead by William Morris. From the 1862 Exhibition onwards Morris was the leading figure who inspired

Walter Crane, a leading figure in the development of the Arts and Crafts movement, defined it as follows:-

'The movement represents in some sense a revolt against the hard mechanical conventional life and its insensitivity to beauty. It is a protest against that so called industrial progress which produces shoddy wares, the cheapness of which is paid for by the lives of their producers and the degradation of their users. It is a protest against the turning of men into machines against artificial distinctions in art, and against making the immediate market value or possibility of profit the chief test of artistic merit. It also advances the claim of all and each to the common possession of beauty in things common and familiar.' [4]

1.6 Design; front cover Guild of Handicraft Catalogue circa 1903

1.7 Oak settle with coved back, decorated with raised gilt gesso, designed by Philip Webb (1831-1915) for Morris & Co.

through his writings, his public speaking and through his remarkable productivity in decorative design. His business attracted commissions to decorate houses of very wealthy patrons, but by the late 1870s The Firm was becoming fashionable amongst the affluent middle classes. The Morris 'look' became easily recognisable from goods displayed in his Oxford Street shop and from printed catalogues which emphasised the importance of good design and the link between historical art and fashionable taste.

After 1875 another shop, Liberty in Regent Street, was beginning to make a powerful influence on taste. Arthur Lazenby Liberty, the proprietor, was an expert on and importer of rare fabrics, shawls, and oriental ware, and became a friend of the artists and aesthetes of the time such as Rossetti, Whistler and Godwin, supplying them with ravishing silks and oriental ware. Liberty is credited as establishing a vogue for what has been described as the visual trimmings of the 'rich sensual world of bohemian aestheticism'.[5]

The particular style and image of Liberty's was presented more as a stylish Art Gallery than a shop, giving customers the experience that they were buying art or being artistic just by being there. Introducing art into shopping was a great achievement for Liberty which to great extent lead the way for other 'artistic home furnishers' particularly Shapland and Petter.

Leading figures at the turn of the century;

Charles Robert Ashbee and the Guild of Handicraft

A significant development in the Arts and Crafts movement was the establishment of the Guild of Handicraft by C.R. Ashbee in 1888. The Guild of Handicraft, which was based initially in Whitechapel in the East End of London, created furniture, metalwork, jewellery and other decorative items for sale in London shops including in later years, their own showroom at 67a Bond Street (Derring Yard), and from 1899, at 15A Brook Street, off Bond Street.

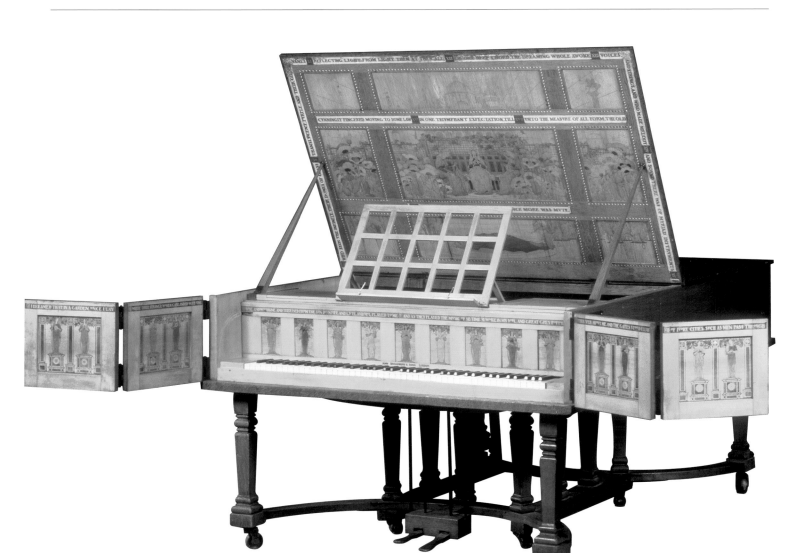

1.8 C. R. Ashbee. Semi-grand piano designed in 1900.

In 1902 Ashbee and the Guild moved to Chipping Campden in the Cotswolds and established a community of craftsmen and their families living and working together. In many respects, the Guild was an experiment in socialism, attempting to create a workers co-operative with shared goals and communal ownership.

As well as leading the Guild, Ashbee also designed some of the finer pieces of furniture in the style that Morris might have called 'state furniture'. In his work he made great play on the decoration of pieces using inlay of different woods and pewter depicting plant forms. His use of elaborate metalwork with long sinuous hinges and lock plates derived from Medieaval forms in which the decoration also served the function of holding the piece together His decorative pieces included enamelled and painted designs, the piano illustrated here being an important example. The Guild of Handicraft also made furniture for other designers, the most celebrated and influential was Baillie Scott.

Mackay Hugh Baillie Scott

Some of the most exuberant and florid examples of decorated furniture were designed by the architect Baillie Scott who was perhaps one of the most influential figures in the Arts and Crafts movement at the turn of the century. Like many of the leading figures in the establishment of the Arts and Crafts movement Baillie Scott was an architect who 'strayed' into the design of furniture. He was a prolific writer who published his designs widely and was also very influential on matters of taste.

Reports of his work in journals such as *The Studio* led to an important commission for the Palace at Darmstadt for the Grand Duke and Duchess of Hesse in 1898. The furniture which he designed was made by the Guild of Handicraft and included highly decorated pieces.

1.9 M.H. Baillie Scott. Design for a music cabinet. The Studio 1898

the Arts Workers Guild in 1884 and his influence gathered strength as he regularly published designs in *The British Architect* from 1888. When *The Studio* magazine was launched in 1893, Voysey was invited to design the front cover, choosing the characters of Use and Beauty holding hands and kissing beneath the boughs of a rose tree.

The Studio became increasingly influential as a bridge between the specialist architectural journals and the artistically inclined general public, featuring the work of Voysey and other Arts and Crafts designers. Furniture and metalwork designed by Voysey was illustrated in the periodicals such as *Furniture and Decoration* and *The Studio,* and at the Arts and Crafts Exhibitions. Through this publicity, his decorative vocabulary of pierced hearts, birds, trees and entwined plant forms as well as his distinctive style of lettering became quietly but firmly established in Arts and Crafts design. Voysey's relationship with God is seen to have influenced his work and his choice of imagery is seen to follow his belief that nature was an expression of God's work.

Whilst the structure of furniture by Baillie Scott shows his concern for proportion and for simple shapes, the striking feature is the decoration. Simple pieces are ornamented lavishly with colour, applied decoration in relief, inlay of coloured woods, ivory, ebony, pewter and pearl. His designs include chequered inlay and geometric or repetitive design but his most florid decoration is of stylised natural forms. His designs for a collection of furniture made by J.P. White in 1901 are illustrated in a catalogue in which he explains that:-

'if ornament is used it is well to make sure that it is thoughtfully conceived and carefully executed and that it at least suggests and reflects in however small a degree some of the beauty of the earth.' [6]

Charles Francis Annesley Voysey

Charles Voysey, the son of a non-conformist minister, was one of the most important influences in the development of Arts and Crafts design. He established his architectural practice in about 1882, and, though primarily concerned with architecture, he developed an interest in decorative arts. Voysey was elected to

1.9 Studio 1903 front cover.

1.11 'Two of Messrs Shapland and Petter new designs'. Furniture and Decoration & the Furniture Gazette Sept 1894

1.11 'Two of Messrs Shapland and Petter new designs'. Furniture and Decoration & the Furniture Gazette Sept 1894

Furniture as Fashion and Art

It is interesting to consider what might have been in the minds of people who followed the fashion for artistic furniture, what motivated them to pay the price and what they felt they had gained from buying into the Arts and Crafts style. An important concept underpinning the growing appetite for the furniture by companies like Shapland and Petter was that people were not just buying furniture for the functions it performed, they were buying it as art. The artistic style and decoration of this furniture signalled modern taste, progressive thinking and moving on from the old Victorian order.

Fashionable Furniture

Clearly the essential ingredients for the broad appeal were the connection with art and with modernity, together these two themes fuelled the fashion. Contemporary adverts and reviews gave great emphasis to manufacturers 'exciting new lines', or the 'very latest designs' as if they were clothes rather than beds, bookcases and wardrobes. As early as 1894 a review of Shapland and Petter emphasised their

'new designs in bedroom suites, tables, sideboards and hall furniture, specially adapted to the requirements of the Autumn season. The whole of the furniture range is characterised by that freshness of design which is peculiar to the firm…' [7]

In 1894 J.S. Henry published his catalogue *Fashionable Furniture* and a review article described it thus:-

'Mr J. S. Henry the well known aesthetic furniture manufacturer of 287-9 Old Street is now issuing a most tasteful and novel little coloured sketch book of new designs… From page to cover it evinces that smartness and 'go' which so characterise fin de Siecle, industrial and pictorial art' [8]

Furnishing the home in the very latest artistic furniture would have been a badge of status for young middle class couples, providing clear evidence of good taste and a cultured lifestyle. These were the very things which the rising middle classes needed for reassurance and confirmation of their status, but another important factor in the success of this style was that it represented 'Art', something that was very much in popular demand by the end of the nineteenth century.

Arts and Crafts Home

The development of Victorian interior design in the late nineteenth century was strongly influenced by artistic aspiration and this was linked to a historical romanticism centred on rural life and the myths of Merrie England. The 'back to the land' movement in the 1890's incorporated interest in folk songs and folk lore with the middle classes reinventing ruralism as a

1.12 The Henry Style. Advertisement J.S. Henry The Studio Vol 39 1907

compensation for city dwelling. Interior design started to reflect traditional style with 'Olde English' honest oak and hand wrought iron or copper.

Within the middle class home, the charm of portraying the Middles Ages could be evoked with the right kind of furniture and decoration. Roy Strong characterises this sensuous dream world or 'never never land of Victorian Medieavalism' [9]

One important factor in understanding the desirability of the Arts and Crafts style was that people buying furniture from Morris or Ashbee for example could identify with the moral virtues of the leading figures. Adrian Forty in *Objects of Desire*[10] raises the concept of 'moral furnishing' with an emphasis on honest construction but also created within an ideological framework of integrity and fairness to the worker and designer. Buying Arts and Crafts style may have signified political as well as artistic aspirations for the middle class buyers.

Out with the old and in with the new

In the latter part of the Victorian era the concept of the modern middle class home was also evolving with a deliberate push to reduce the amount of furniture and clutter in rooms and create more space. Out went heavily upholstered furniture with tassels and bows and fringes in favour of white painted or plain wood framed furniture with loose cushions. Wall to wall carpets were replaced with wood floors and rugs. Casual informality, lightness and fresh air were considered aesthetically and hygienically essential.

Artistic furnishings may well have had a strong appeal for young married couples, setting up home for the first time. The freshness of the designs probably appealed particularly to women who were taking more of a role in interior decoration than their mothers had done.

Home sweet home

The development of industry and commerce during the Victorian period also affected the relationship between home and work, separating the two for many people who had formerly worked from home either in crafts or in business.

As Adrian Forty put it :-

'The home therefore came to be regarded as a repository of the virtues that were lost or denied in the world outside. To the middle classes in the nineteenth century the home stood for feeling, for sincerity, honesty truth and love.' [11]

Home as a place which was the opposite of work could sustain dreams of a different way of life. A fantasy world or a 'heaven' was conceivable and decoration, furniture and design could help to set the stage for the imagination to return to a different and better world. Thus the charm of the country cottage or medieaval hall or Camelot, was for many the preferred theme for their ideal home, and the furniture manufacturers were pleased to oblige with the appropriate props.

An interesting trend in marketing Arts and Crafts furniture at the turn of the century was to give names to individual pieces. Liberty were particularly fond of this practice using names of

1.13 C.F.A. Voysey design for a writing cabinet; portrayal of a rural idyll with heart motifs. V&A E.274-1913

villages such as Milverton or Compton to name a sideboard or magazine rack. Heals too joined in the romantic labelling with strong cues to artistic settings suggested in their Newlyn and St Ives ranges of bedroom furniture. Shapland and Petter resisted this trend to name individual pieces, though they did adopt an important local historical figure Sir Walter Raleigh as their trade mark and used his name for their new state of the art Raleigh Cabinet Works which we shall see in the next chapter.

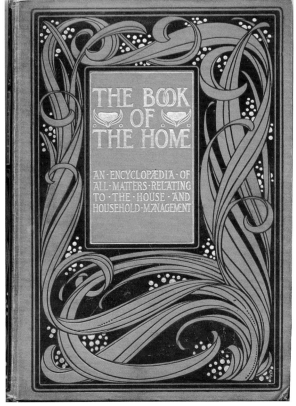

1.14 Book of The Home. Cover design 1904.

1.15 Oak hall robe with copper panels

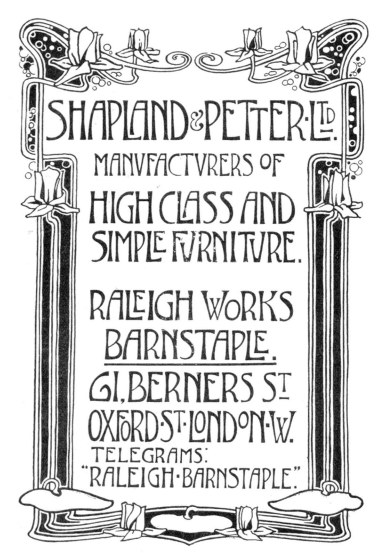

SHAPLAND & PETTER LTD.
MANUFACTURERS OF
HIGH CLASS AND
SIMPLE FURNITURE.

RALEIGH WORKS
BARNSTAPLE.
61, BERNERS ST.
OXFORD ST. LONDON·W.
TELEGRAMS:
"RALEIGH·BARNSTAPLE."

FURNITURE FOR THE

Hall, Bedroom, and Reception Rooms.

LARGE STOCKS READY.

MANTELS, OVERMANTELS, HOUSE FITMENTS,
BANK AND OTHER COUNTERS.

OFFICE FITTINGS.

1.16 *Shapland and Petter Advertisement. Furniture Record. September 1902*

Chapter 2 The Raleigh Cabinet Works

2.1 Oak bureau with inlaid panel and wavy moulded edge. R1529

1529 Bureau. 3 ft 2. inlaid

An appreciation of the work of Shapland and Petter requires some understanding of the background to cabinet making in the Victorian era, and some time to consider the contradictions between the Arts and Crafts tradition and the use of machines to manufacture furniture.

Shapland and Petter made furniture in a mode of production which kept the firm economically viable for the whole of the Victorian and Edwardian period, and their social and economic contribution was highly significant to the people of North Devon. Their innovative approach to the introduction of machinery meant that furniture could be produced at a cost which many people could afford, rather than be restricted to the rich. Their marketing techniques and business organisation kept the firm viable and profitable whilst others closed down. Their wide range of furniture and distribution networks generated a wide base of customers from London to the South Coast, to Glasgow and abroad in Europe.

Machinery in Cabinet Making

Within the foundations of the Arts and Crafts movement, perhaps the strongest standpoint was the opposition to machinery and industrialisation. In *The Stones of Venice* Ruskin argued against the perfection which machines created at the expense of human dignity:-

'Examine again all those accurate mouldings and unerring adjustments of the seasoned wood and tempered steel. Many a time you have exulted over them and thought how great England was because her slightest work was done so thoroughly. Alas, if we read rightly these perfectnesses are the signs of a slavery in our England a thousand times more bitter and degrading than that of the scourged African or helot Greek.' [12]

Industrialisation came relatively late to cabinet making which had been a crafts industry relying on handwork except for some components which could be made by water or steam powered lathes and saws. Until 1860 cabinet making is reported to have been less affected by industrialisation than other branches of decorative arts. The Select Committee of the School of Design, in 1849, heard evidence from pottery, metal, wallpaper, textile manufacturers but made no comment on furniture since there were only two large firms of cabinet makers, most of the trade being individual craftsmen or small firms. [13] As firms grew, with the population explosion from the 1850's, more and more mechanisation was introduced. The large cabinet maker Holland and Sons spent £1250 on machinery in 1857, and Jackson and Graham in 1862 advertised:-

'The Extensive Manufactory adjoining the Machinery, worked by steam power is fitted with all means and appliances to ensure superiority and economise cost.' [14]

Some years before this, Henry Shapland started his own business in Barnstaple which relied upon an ingenious machine that seems to have been unique in England or at least undiscovered by the rest of the cabinet making industry in Britain until years later.

Henry Shapland and the wavy moulding machine

Henry Shapland was born in 1823, the second son of William Shapland, bread baker of Queen Street, Barnstaple in North Devon. He went to the town's Bluecoat School until the age of ten, and was later apprenticed to John Crook, a local cabinet maker. Here he continued working after completing his training and then went to London. He was not successful there, being made redundant from one job, and walking out on another in which he worked making packing cases for fourteen hours a day for less than a living wage. In 1847 while living in London, he married his first wife, a Barnstaple lady. He returned to his home town soon afterwards where he set up a home for his wife. He sailed from Cardiff in October 1847 for America to 'seek his fortune' and discovered the revolution which was taking place across the Atlantic in cabinet making. In America, the 'land of modern mechanical invention' woodworking machinery was fast replacing the laborious preliminary stages of sawing and planing timber. The use of machinery left the skilled men free for the important final stages of assembly and finishing. For the rest of his life Henry Shapland was committed to this concept of manufacturing and was a major pioneer in acquiring and employing the very best in machinery and technology.

While in America he was interested to see a carving machine invented by a German which could produce finely carved moulding on curved surfaces, saving hours of time for the craftsman carver. The machine was worked in secret by its inventor but Shapland persuaded the man to allow him to see and draw the invention, on condition that he promised he would not set up in competition.

Returning to North Devon, Shapland set up in business for himself. By March 1851, at the age of twenty-seven, the census returns show that he was living in the Pilton area of Barnstaple with his wife and two children, describing himself as an 'ornamental moulding maker employing one man'. He set up his first workshop in a small room in an old water powered woollen mill at Raleigh, near Barnstaple, where he reconstructed the machine seen in America. After a short while he moved to Bear

Street near the centre of the town. From his small 'factory' Shapland and his only helper George Trevesick, who laboriously turned the handle to power the lathe, started to manufacture mouldings, initially to sell to piano manufacturers in London.

By 1854 Shapland had employed Henry Petter, a Barnstaple man who returned from London where he had worked in the publishing trade as a partner in Cassell, Petter & Galpin, still trading today as Cassells. Petter acted as a travelling salesman for

2.2 Shapland and Petter Works outing. Circa 1900. Museum of Barnstaple and North Devon

Barnstaple as an industrial town

For over a thousand years Barnstaple has been the most important town in North Devon due to two main factors.

The first is its position at the lowest fordable point on the River Taw and more importantly – giving access to the Bristol Channel and beyond. For centuries Barnstaple was a busy trading port where rich merchants made fortunes importing goods from Europe, Africa and America. Unfortunately the river gradually silted up during the eighteenth and nineteenth centuries, until by the 1850s only coasting vessels could trade there and all ocean-going trade ceased.

The second important factor in the economic growth of Barnstaple was its involvement in the wool trade. Devon was a county of sheep and abundant streams and rivers. The wool required many labour intensive processes between shearing and making into cloth and running water was also vital. The many water-mills in and around Barnstaple were busy in the woollen trade, the largest of which was at Raleigh, just outside the town. However, by the eighteenth century this trade was in decline for various reasons with great hardship resulting for all involved. By the 1850s this mill and many others were no longer major employers. Although lace-making and gloving were local industries, they could not absorb the large numbers of desperate paupers in the town. When Henry Shapland was offered the tenancy of this abandoned building early in the 1850s, complete with a row of workers' cottages and a constant supply of free power courtesy of the nearby River Yeo, he was quick to grasp his chance. The lack of employment in Barnstaple meant that he had no problem in recruiting men willing to learn a useful trade and within twenty years a hundred families were surviving on wages earned at the Raleigh Cabinet Works. The firm is still successfully trading with a workforce of several hundred people.

the firm, and also invested money in the enterprise. Complete furniture as well as mouldings was being manufactured in Bear Street and sold in Barnstaple High Street and elsewhere, and through Petter's contacts and business acumen, furniture of quality was being sold widely to the trade. In 1864 the firm moved back to Raleigh, encouraged by Shapland's old Sunday School teacher, Mr Maunder, who had retired from running a woollen mill there. By 1870 over a hundred men were employed at the Raleigh Cabinet Works, still powered by two enormous water wheels, one of 22 feet and the other of 20 feet. Henry Shapland, remembering his experiences in America in the 1840s, was convinced of the need to make use of the latest labour-saving woodworking machinery – which initially meant buying from across the Atlantic.

However, England too had its inventors and in 1867 *Building News* reported on the invention of a machine by Mr Robert Thompson who had previously been in charge of woodworking machinery at HM Dockyard at Woolwich. This new machine was said to be "*readily adapted for cutting curvilinear and other shaped mouldings in wood and also finishing and polishing same... and will accomplish as much work as 25 skilled workmen in the same period of time.*"[15] This sounds very much like the machine which Shapland had created in Barnstaple more than ten years earlier.

Shapland and Petter: The Raleigh Cabinet Works

Shapland continued to develop his business selling to London customers and in 1865 took Henry Petter into partnership, accepting from him £800 as capital. Petter, a former publisher and fellow member of the Plymouth Brethren, brought important skills in marketing, and the company began to grow, making high quality furniture for the London retailers. By 1872 the firm has grown sufficiently for the North Devon Journal to report on the annual works outing:

'Employer's Treat On Saturday last the employees of Messrs Shapland and Petter of the Raleigh works to the number of nearly 100, had their annual day out, Exmouth on this occasion being the place selected. Arrangements were made with the London and South Western Railway Company for a special train to and fro, leaving Barnstaple at 7.30 am and arriving at Exmouth at 10 am. They were catered for at The Dolphin, luncheon being prepared on arrival and a capital diner served at half past two.' [16]

We are very fortunate to have an account of the Raleigh Cabinet Works from *Strong's Industries of North Devon* which in 1889 gave an excellent description of the early history of the firm and detail of the new works established after fire destroyed their original premises at Raleigh.[17] From the start of the company, Shapland had shown a fascination with machinery. America was

2.3 Advertisement for Raleigh Cabinet Works. Furniture Record 1905

seen to have applied machinery to so many woodworking operations and he was keen to invest in this latest machinery.

'Messrs Shapland and Petter were among the firms who resolved to avail themselves of these great labour saving appliances. They gave instructions to the agent of Messrs J.A. Fay and Co of Cincinnati, Ohio to fit up a most complete set of woodworking machinery... Shapland and Petter were continually adding novelties peculiar to their manufactures as soon as the ingenuity of the inventive mind had sought out and produced 'some new thing'...'[18]

A stroke of fate which forced Shapland and Petter to relocate and modernise came in the form of a disastrous fire in March 1888 which completely destroyed their premises, workshop, their stock and the workmen's own tools which were stored at the factory. Fires were not unusual in the furniture making trade,

Wylie and Lochhead, furniture makers in Glasgow, also suffered similarly with a serious fire, as did many other companies working in wood at this time.[19] For Shapland and Petter the fire prompted an immediate response to rebuild and modernise the business, preventing economic ruin, and the loss of social capital which might have occurred if skilled men had drifted off to find work elsewhere.

'Almost ere the lurid glare had departed from the ruins which had replaced a splendid industry, when silence and darkness had fallen the scene of the busy hum of machinery and the movement of clever craftsmen plying their decorative arts... the foundation stone of the new manufactory had been laid... Messages had been flashed to America, by the Atlantic Cable, securing machinery which it was impossible to obtain in the Old Country and orders were given at home for all the necessities of a new industry.'[20]

The New Raleigh Cabinet Works at Bridge Wharf

Within weeks of the fire Shapland and Petter had created a 'new and modern manufactory' at Bridge Wharf on the River Taw near the centre of Barnstaple. The land had been a shipbuilding yard which they had acquired a year earlier and it presented an ideal location with road, rail and sea links to suppliers and customers world wide.

A key consideration in the design and construction was safety, particularly fire prevention, and every modern appliance was provided including the 'Grinnel Automatic Sprinkler', with a complete system of water supply through ten hydrants located in different parts of the buildings. Constructed in widely separated blocks, each contained floors which were solidly constructed of concrete or three inch planks 'without any apertures to serve as flues', stairs and lift wells were outside of the building or separate from workshops. Another ingenious safeguard to extract sawdust was the Cyclone *'which has scarcely an equal in its mechanical appointments throughout the whole of Europe.'* And finally the light:-

'The electric light is another element of safety. The whole of the workshops are lit with this brilliant and safe illuminant; and a pretty and novel sight it is to catch, from across the river, a glimpse of the whole block a glow with the light electricity has given us.'[21]

In *Strong's Industries of North Devon* a description of the existing and planned set-up for the workshops was presented. A sawmill was planned for Block A in which circular saws, bandsaws and saw sharpening machines were installed. A log bandsaw, the first of its kind in the country, was also installed, capable of cutting logs up to five feet in diameter at rapid speed. The sawmill was situated next to the wharf and the river, convenient for loading to and from ships, and a railway line ran through the yard and the mill.

2.4 Cabinet Makers Shop at Shapland and Petter circa 1900 Museum of Barnstaple and North Devon

2.5 Cabinet makers and apprentices of Shapland and Petter circa 1900. Museum of Barnstaple and North Devon.

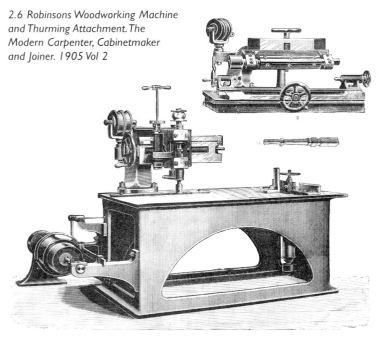

2.6 Robinsons Woodworking Machine and Thurming Attachment. The Modern Carpenter, Cabinetmaker and Joiner. 1905 Vol 2

2.7 A donkey machine, circa 1920, it is assumed that earlier or similar versions of this machine were used in the works before the turn on the century, given the large output of inlaid work

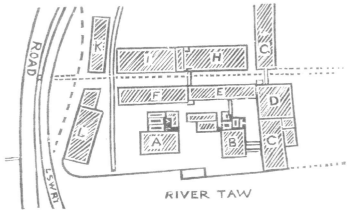

2.8 Plan of the Raleigh Cabinet Works, Strong H.W. 1889

In Block B there were the drying kilns where wood could be perfectly seasoned in twelve days as opposed to two or more years if dried naturally. This innovation was developed by Henry Shapland's son, Richard Arthur. The wood was stacked in air tight chambers lined with absorbent felt where a temperature of 120 degrees was maintained. After some hours of 'sweating', steam was injected into the chamber and circulated before being sucked out by powerful fans then forced through cold condensers to remove the moisture. This circulation took place thousands of times a day and continued until all the wood was dry.

The power for the factory came from Block C which housed two boilers, a powerful 'Lancashire' and a locomotive capable of developing 100 horsepower at 200 revolutions per minute. This power was multiplied up to create up to 6000 revolutions per minute for some of the cutting machines. Another engine running at 300 revolutions, self lubricating, and a dynamo to generate electricity completed the 'motive power' for the factory.

In handling the wood in the early stages of its processing an *"ingenious labour saving contrivance,"* was used, the original conception of Mr R. A. Shapland:-

'Oblique elevators reach across the yard... each conveying boards to different floors of the dry wood store. Pairs of endless chains, driven by chain wheels, form an ever travelling table, upon which the boards

are placed at the lower end to be received on the floor upon which the higher end of the elevator is placed... Three men are busily employed in taking in the incessant supply of this capable carrier.' [22]

In Block D, wood was selected for initial machining under the watchful eye of the foreman, Mr Seyfert, who had a staff of twenty men working under him. The timber was carefully selected for various kinds of work and then passed on to 'liners' who marked it off into sizes and indicated its destination in particular pieces of furniture. Every piece of wood in every item of furniture would be numbered, cut to shape with circular saws, and passed down to the next floor where 'jointing up' took place.

The machinery department in Block E housed two machines for joining up lengths of timber to the required widths, and the work would then be passed to a planing machine for *"flat surfacing, thicknessing, and planing at various angles."* The department housed high speed mortising machines, one English and one American, and a *"remarkable tenoning"* machine which could cut four sides of wood at once . In addition there were the spindle moulding machines:-

'In this splendidly appointed machine room there were... machines for 'thurming' or what is more familiarly termed square moulded work, for rebating, grooving &c. To add to the completeness of the mechanical means of manufacture we must catalogue the presence

2.9 Shapland and Petter Lorry circa 1920. Museum of Barnstaple and North Devon

on the same floor of three double spindle vertical moulding machines, for working mouldings on the edge of wide surfaces either straight or to any irregular shape. The machines are also used for producing shaped work of any design to a pattern on which the work is fixed'[23]

On the top floor of Block E was a knife grinder and tool sharpener, horizontal and vertical boring machines and others for squaring up work, a dovetailing machine, and machines for

cross dovetailing and sand papering. On the ground floor, turning lathes, square moulding machines and thurming cylinders were housed. The veneering department also shared some of this accommodation.

Veneering was carried out by a large and separate team of workmen. Pieces of figured wood were matched and joined and 'manipulated so as to produce striking effects'. Immense quantities of glue were used in this department and:-

'Great iron presses in which as many as twenty sets of veneer are laid out at the same time and in contrast to these ponderous appliances, here also are seen tiniest saws at work, almost invisible in their movements; they are employed in letting and filling the various holes and defects in the veneer, so perfectly are these inlaid that it is almost impossible to detect the piecing.' [24]

It is assumed that the marquetry and inlaying work was carried out in a workshop attached or near to the veneering department because of the need for access to veneers and also the need for presses and cutting equipment. The process of cutting multiple pieces of inlay of identical shape was most probably managed by the use of a particular machine called a

2.10 Unloading Timber at Bridge Wharf, early twentieth century. Museum of Barnstaple and North Devon

'donkey'. Henry Percy Shapland, the grandson of the founder, illustrates this machine used for cutting inlay, in his book on decoration of furniture.[25] The 'donkey' was a hand made saw fixed on a bench upon which the marquetry cutters sat. A foot clamp was fitted which enabled cutters to hold and cut several layers of veneer to create identical pieces. See 2.7.

Block F housed *'a great number of different kinds of sawing machines'* and Block H top floor stored work which had been machined and was waiting to be given out to the cabinet makers for fitting and finishing. On the same floor in Block H was the carvers department.

'Among the numbers of carvers employed by the firm there are exceptionally clever craftsmen. The carver working in wood the type of man working out his destiny imparts a romantic cast to the thought of the visitor. Mr Williams Green has control of this craft, issuing the working drawings from which the finer suites of furniture display, some very fine carvings are produced.' [26]

Cabinet makers worked in Blocks H and I and the assembled work was passed on to the examiners of the work, Messrs Gabriel and James, who then passed it on to the polishing department. From here the completed work was sent to a packing and forwarding department and then to be loaded onto railway trucks or motor lorry.

Other processes and workshops were also important; the marble working department cut, shaped and polished marble tops for hall stands, and bedroom wash stands and there were also the fumigating rooms.:-

'When the basement block is approached, a strong ammoniacal odour excites the olfactory organs of the visitor… The strong aroma is emitted from the fumigating rooms where oak and mahogany are place for the purpose of bringing their hue to the required shade. The fumigation process has the same effect upon the wood as age.' [27]

Arts and Crafts workshops, photographic and design studio

Unfortunately there appear to be no records of the workshops which produced the Arts and Crafts metalwork, specifically the repoussé copper panels for which Shapland and Petter are renowned. We know from contemporary reviews of the company that copper work and enamelling was carried out at the works (see Chapter 5) but no trace of information has yet been found at the works site or in the archive. As well as producing panels, there may have been other metalwork produced on site, possibly the hand wrought handles and hinges which have not been found with any manufacturer mark and are clearly hand made items. See 5.11.

The stencilling, painted work and embroidery may well have been carried out off-site as this craft work was particularly suitable for home working, or this may have been included in another workshop. No location is given for the design room which employed several staff from the late 1890s onwards, nor is any mention given to the photographic studio or showrooms which records indicate were in existence after 1900.

Importing Timber

The new Raleigh Cabinet Works of Shapland and Petter which came into being in 1888 was in an ideal situation geographically being on a navigable river. From their wharf on the River Taw in Barnstaple, Shapland and Petter was in easy reach of Plymouth, Southampton, Portsmouth, Bristol and Cardiff, ports for importing timber from across the world and exporting finished goods to America and Europe. Cargoes of timber could be unloaded to their wharf right alongside the factory yard to be sawn and dried. There are also reports from local historians of huge logs being floated or towed up the river Taw and beached for up to two or three years near the factory where they waited to be hauled to the saw mill when they were needed.

In the company archive there are references to the local vessels such as the *Bessie Gould* which brought timber from London and Chepstow from about 1893, and mention also of the Bideford and Bristol Steam Navigation Co and other local shipping companies.

Evidence of timber imported from more distant sources is recorded in the accounts which show references to timber from Frederickstadt in Norway, Buenos Aires, South Africa, and Canada. The accounts record in 1895 freight timber from Montreal, in 1896 from Quebec. In 1900 cargoes are recorded from the West Indies, Mexico, much via the Elder Dempster Line and Glyn & Son which included walnut, rosewood, cherrywood, oak, poplar, ash, mulberry, mahogany, birch and chestnut. The accounts show regular payments to ships' captains or masters in payment for timber and occasionally for 'Ale Money'. Ships named in the records as well as the *Bessie Gould*, include the *Dictator, Monteagle* and *Brooklyn City*.

As well as fairly large scale importing of timber Shapland and Petter also made the best of opportunities to buy timber locally. Accounts show payments for home grown timber bought locally from Burrington, Fortescue Estates, Nethercott & Bishops Tawton, sometimes even for individual trees. Carl. J. Seyfert was the timber foreman for Shapland and Petter at the turn of the century and responsible for buying local timber in Devon and Somerset. He is recorded as visiting the Fortescue Estates and others to inspect standing timber and to negotiate the purchase

2.11 Fumed oak hall chair R1036, and hall stand with copper panel

21

of logs. The ledger recorded the purchase of cherry, pollard oak and walnut in 1895. Henry Shapland himself also made many trips to see and buy timber in England and Wales as well as trips to America, South Africa and Europe.

As a provincial furniture maker, Shapland and Petter was able to benefit from the traditional seafaring and trading links from Barnstaple to a wide range of ports across the western world for importing and exporting. Developing their international network showed an adventurousness and business acumen which Henry Shapland had demonstrated earlier in his trip to America. This entrepreneurial drive helped the company develop their skill and technology as importers of timber, and this must have given them some economic advantage over other furniture makers who had to pay wholesalers and timber importers. Importing their own timber also meant that Shapland and Petter could be sure of picking the very best timber with complete control over its processing for fine cabinet making. The development of their business as a supplier of timber and veneers also helped to increase income and consolidate the economic strength of the company.

Industry or machine assisted craft?

We are fortunate to have a contemporary account, albeit incomplete, of the scenes and smells inside the workshops of Shapland and Petter at the turn of the century.[28] Clearly, they were one of the leading companies in the mechanisation of furniture making. Their commercial success was evident in that they supported through their business a large workforce of trained and highly skilled people. In 1900 they were employing approximately 400 people in the business, compared to the largest company, Lebus in London employing about 1000 people.

A contrast can be drawn between the manufacturing cabinet makers such as Shapland and Petter and smaller firms or workshops within the Arts and Crafts movement around the turn of the century. The Guild of Handicraft for example employed about seventy men at the Silk Mill in Chipping Campden working on a range of metalwork and crafts. The Newlyn School of Industrial Arts in Cornwall and the Moorcroft Factory in Staffordshire may each have involved twenty people or less, and individual craftsmen such Gimson and the Barnsleys worked alone or in small workshops designing and hand making their furniture with few powered machines.

There has been perhaps, an unwarranted level of criticism of commercially manufactured furniture, on the assumption that the principles of Arts and Crafts had been compromised through the use of machinery and the integrity of the craftsman lost in the industrial setting of the factory. Whilst the Arts and Crafts

movement was founded in a reaction against industrialisation, the leading exponents did come to accept the value of machinery in craft work. Morris, for example, appeared to have been forced to reconsider his attitudes to machine production during the 1880s and by 1884 he was quoted as praising:-

'Those almost miraculous machines, which if orderly forethought had dealt with them might even now be speedily extinguishing all irksome and unintelligent labour, leaving us free to raise the standard of skill of hand and the energy of mind in our workmen.'[29]

Ashbee too, was prepared to accept the value of machinery in the workshop, provided it brought satisfaction to the craftsman as well as to the consumer. However as Shapland and Petter embraced their new technology, it appears that Ashbee did not and in the early years of the twentieth century, as the Guild of Handicraft struggled to survive economically, Ashbee cast around for reasons for this failure and complained of the *'fashion for antiques churned out in hundreds to the hum of the latest American Machinery'.*[30]

One of the key factors in the success of Shapland and Petter was undoubtedly their use of machinery but it is essential to recognise and give full credit to the skill and craftsmanship which were involved in the creation of their Arts and Crafts furniture. Furniture historian Clive Edwards has clearly demonstrated the case that furniture making in the latter part of the Victorian period was a 'machine assisted craft' rather than an industry dominated by machines.[31] At the turn of the century the Raleigh Cabinet Works represented a bridge between the traditional craft workshop and the new style furniture factory, where elements of the old and the new sat side by side. What is important is that Shapland and Petter provided the technological and commercial conditions to enable their craftsmen to learn and develop craft skills and work at their trade, father and son, in long term employment. Their progressive approach and business acumen helped the craft of cabinet making to survive and flourish, and the fruits of their endeavours are among the finest examples of furniture in the Arts and Crafts style.

Chapter 3 Arts and Crafts in the Commercial World

3.1 Inside Cover Guild of Handicraft Catalogue, circa 1903

SOME of the best craftsmen in this country, in their respective crafts, are employed in the Guild workshops, and in the following pages will be found illustrations and prices of articles made in the various departments, comprising :—

GOLD AND SILVERSMITHING	WOOD CARVING
JEWELLERY	BLACKSMITHING
ENAMELS	ELECTRICAL FITTINGS
ECCLESIASTICAL ORNAMENTS	PLASTER WORK
FURNITURE	HOUSE DECORATION

Amongst others who have entrusted the Guild with important commissions, or for whom work has been carried out, may be mentioned the following :—

H.M. THE QUEEN	THE MARQUIS OF LANSDOWNE	LADY PENRHYN
THE GRAND DUKE OF HESSE	EARL BEAUCHAMP	LADY HORNBY
THE DUCHESS OF LEEDS	THE EARL OF GAINSBOROUGH	LADY MURIEL PAGET
THE COUNTESS OF PORTSMOUTH	LORD BALCARRES	THE HON. MRS. GOSCHEN
THE COUNTESS OF IDDESLEIGH	THE MACINTOSH OF MACINTOSH	MRS. BEERBOHM TREE
THE COUNTESS BATHURST	LORD REDESDALE	MRS. PATRICK CAMPBELL
LADY ELCHO	LORD BRAYE	MR. FORBES ROBERTSON
LADY KINTORE	THE BISHOP OF LONDON	MR. E. S. WILLARD
LADY ROBERT CECIL	THE BISHOP OF DURHAM	ETC.

J. MILES & CO., LTD.,
68 & 70, WARDOUR STREET, W.

In 2004 the Leaderflush Shapland company[32] celebrated its 150 year Anniversary, tracing its origins back through several mergers and reconfigurations to the original Raleigh Cabinet Works in Barnstaple. As we know now, Shapland and Petter started with a single entrepreneur, Henry Shapland, a small workshop and a 'wage slave', George Trevisick, to turn the handle of the wavy moulding machine. This simple business which started 20 years before Liberty opened in his shop in Regent Street in 1875, thrived and grew under the direction of Shapland and Petter and there are a number of factors which helped their commercial success.

In his very thorough analysis of the Victorian furniture trade, Clive Edwards emphasises how slowly industrialisation reached the cabinet making business.[33] Factors which slowed its progress were the abundance of labour, and the complex nature of cabinet making in craft orientated workshops where assembly by hand was the most important activity. The role of the machine as an enabling mechanism was important in economic growth but not as a single determining factor in the creation and survival of companies like Shapland and Petter. Other factors, particularly the concentration of different stages in production under one roof were essential, and the 'vertical' integration of the process

of sourcing raw materials and marketing the finished product to the customer were also vitally important. This chapter looks at the commercial factors, from the business ethos and acumen, to the advertising, marketing and distribution networks at which Shapland and Petter excelled. These were the crucial factors which made them a major force in bringing Arts and Crafts to the new markets, enabling them to keep pace with the leading companies in London and elsewhere.

The Paradox of the Arts and Crafts Business

The need to generate income to pay the wages of craftsmen and to finance the 'business' of producing was one of the central challenges for producers working within the Arts and Crafts movement at the turn of the century.

Whilst the leading thinkers such as Morris, Burges and Ashbee were men from wealthy families, the workers in their workshops needed to be paid every week and this meant finding customers, selling products and making profit in the commercial market. Opposition to industrialisation was fine in theory but the return to Guilds and to individual craftsmanship created expensive hand made products which only the rich could afford. See for example some of the wealthy customers of the Guild of Handicraft 3.1.

CHRISTMAS PRESENTS

The Woodbury Gallery

37, NEW BOND ST., W.

NOW OPEN   ADMISSION FREE

An IMPORTANT EXHIBITION

OF THE WORK OF THE

Guild of Handicraft

DRAWINGS
SKETCHES
DESIGNS
GOLD AND
SILVER WORK
JEWELLERY
FURNITURE
PIANOS
PRINTED
BOOKS
ENAMELS

A Workshop of the Guild of Handicraft, Campden, Glos.

The Work of the
following is
represented:

C. R. ASHBEE
WM. STRANG
REGINALD
    SAVAGE
C. R. BAKER
GEO. THOMPSON
EDITH
   HARWOOD
ANNA
   KINGSFORD

&c., &c.

In addition to the Exhibition of the work of the Guild, a fine
collection of Woodbury Reproductions of Old & Modern Masters
is on view. ∅ ∅ Catalogue of 1,500 works reproduced in Carbon
and other Art Processes, 1s, post free

3.2 Guild of Handicraft Exhibition Advertisement. Connoisseur. 1902 no16

Both Ruskin and William Morris died frustrated men, having spent their lives trying to bring about social and artistic reform to a largely indifferent public. Whilst they carried their banner in the name of humanity, the new society that they envisaged bore little relationship to the average person, its relevance being confined to an appreciative, affluent, and intelligent elite.

William Morris, as a socialist reformer aspired to *'Art for All'* but he realised that much of his efforts had been consumed in *'Ministering luxury to the swinish rich'* rather than creating the means to bring art to good citizens of a more humble status.[34] Ashbee too became disillusioned as the Guild of Handicraft failed to balance the books in 1907, and after the Guild was wound up he reflected later that:-

'We have made of a great social movement, a narrow and tiresome aristocracy, working with great skill for the very rich.'[35]

In contrast to Ashbee's Guild, Shapland and Petter were able to produce high quality hand finished furniture in an economical way and supply it to people across the country, widening the interest in the movement and enabling more people to benefit, as craftsmen and employees in a sustainable company, and on the other side of the factory gate, as a wide network of consumers.

Arts & Crafts, Brethren & Commerce

Before considering the practical business of marketing, it is important to understand the ideological and religious context in which the business was created and sustained, as this too was an important factor in success. In this section, Dr Roger Shuff has provided us with assistance in an understanding of the religious beliefs and practices of the founders.[36]

Recording his personal memories of Henry Shapland and Henry Petter, Ernest Shapland more than hinted at the fundamental significance of their faith to this joint commercial venture: *'He and my father were Plymouth Brethren, and both were all their subsequent lives. Henry Petter suggested to my father that he should sell his furniture from drawings and coloured sketches and offered him his capital, amounting to £800 to him in return for a partnership.'*[37]

On the one hand Shapland and Petter were Nonconformist entrepreneurs whose activities echoed on a smaller scale those of such exponents of Victorian capitalism as the Congregational Lord Leverhulme, soap manufacturer of Port Sunlight and founder of Unilever, or the Baptist J.J. Colman, the Norwich mustard producer.

The devout Christianity that marked Nonconformists has long been recognised historically as a driving force of capitalism. On the other hand Shapland's and Petter's particular beliefs as Brethren had an innate affinity with significant elements of the Arts and Crafts ethos. This distinctive blend of outlook would have lain behind the effectiveness with which they were able to marry shrewd commercial practice with genuine hand craftsmanship.

Both the Arts and Crafts and the Brethren movements were, in fact, products of the Romantic mood that informed the thinking of William Wordsworth, Samuel Taylor Coleridge and numerous others in the early nineteenth century. Their literary work was permeated with the desire to escape the upward, yet to their mind soulless march of humanity that had been championed by rational Enlightenment philosophers in the previous century. In place of this, the urge was to rediscover awareness of the emotional and spiritual aspects of life, finding inspiration through the observation of nature, leading to a sense of worship that reached beyond it.

The Arts and Crafts movement and the Brethren movement (often referred to as the 'Plymouth' Brethren because their first congregation in England was in Plymouth), can therefore be seen as parallel movements. The Arts and Crafts movement had at its root radical thinkers such as John Ruskin, Thomas Carlyle and William Morris who were disillusioned with so-called 'progress' in the form of rampant industrialisation, and promoted a return to the purer values and primitive craftsmanship thought to have held sway before the creative spirit of the individual had been stifled by an oppressive regime of mechanisation and mass-production in pursuit of profit.

The pioneers of the Brethren movement were, in turn, radical Protestant Nonconformists disillusioned with the existing state of religion which they regarded as institutionalised and narrow-minded. Important Brethren leaders - notably J.N. Darby (1800-1882), an Anglo-Irish aristocrat and clergyman - promoted a return to the 'primitive' Christianity of the New Testament before the Christian Church became formalised into structures and hierarchies that stifled a more authentic and spontaneous spirit in divine worship. By the time the Shapland and Petter business was established, the Darbyite stream of Brethren to which they belonged had established a close-knit network of inter-related congregations throughout the British Isles and around the world. (This was in contrast to the other section of the movement commonly known as 'open' Brethren where local churches were independent of each other.)

The potential significance from a commercial viewpoint of Shapland and Petter's connection with a burgeoning religious group of this nature should not be overlooked. Indeed, it is probable that their mutual Brethren interest played a key role in bringing Henry Shapland and Henry Petter together in the first instance. Moreover, the formative role played by Shapland's former Sunday School teacher and business mentor, Mr Maunder (see chapter 2), may possibly have come about through this new religious movement which was attracting adherents and affirming relationships of trust and respect between people from a variety of backgrounds.

To an established business, therefore, membership of this Brethren network could undoubtedly prove beneficial in areas like personnel, finance, supply of materials and sales. In addition to members of the second (and possibly third) generation of the Shapland and Petter families, key employees were fellow Brethren members at Rackfield Hall, their place of worship. These are known to have included Carl J. Seyfert, timber foreman; William Cowie, the Scottish designer and draughtsman who headed up the firm's Design Room, as well as his son, Robert Cowie, a salesman who was travelling for the firm well into the twentieth century. Religious meetings for employees to attend (presumably on a voluntary basis) were held regularly at the works. Further research is required to understand the extent to which Brethren contacts provided financial support to the firm, particularly in more difficult times, and represented significant suppliers of raw materials from abroad as well as at home.

Marketing

A very important factor in the growth and strength of the Shapland and Petter company was their skill at marketing their products. Their technical innovation and shrewd exploitation of their position to import timber must have helped significantly but finding people to buy their products was the key to success. The company showed great commercial ability in establishing a network of shops and suppliers to sell their products and most importantly they were able to produce illustrated catalogues to tempt buyers, to compete with, and to sell to companies such as Liberty, Waring and Gillows and Wylie and Lochhead. As well as producing a seemingly infinite range of furniture supplied to retailers shops country wide, they could sell directly to the customer from their own 'high class' shop in London's West End. More than just a provincial cabinet maker, Shapland and Petter were, at the turn of the century, among the grand masters of manufacturing home furnishers.

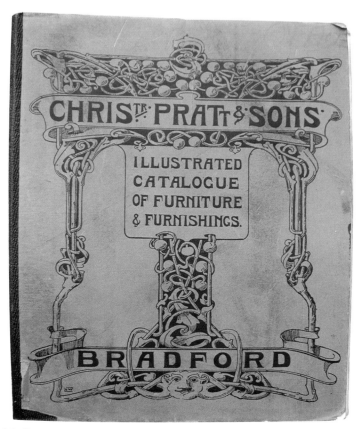

3.3 Christopher Pratt and Sons. Bradford Catalogue. 1901 WYAS. 46D95/6/1

Selling the Image: Catalogues as a marketing tool

Catalogues became an important marketing tool for furniture manufacturers, and an essential part of the marketing strategy for well known companies such as Liberty's which produced over 100 catalogues between 1881 and the launch of their *Inexpensive Furniture Catalogue* in 1907. Catalogues were popular a long time before Liberty's however, Heals were advertising their range of beds in railway advertisements and in the covers of books by Charles Dickens in 1845. 1840s trade directories listed a number of men as artists working in furniture making districts and design books were published by them, some volumes slight others substantial. The catalogue of William Smee in 1855 is recorded to have had 600 designs and the largest was that of Sewell and Sewell with over 1000 pages.[38]

In the Arts and Crafts style, early catalogues included Collinson and Lock's *Sketches of Artistic Furniture*, then that of William Watt who published his catalogue of *Art Furniture* in 1877. By the 1880s Liberty were producing catalogues of *Yuletide Gifts and Artistic Novelties*, and in 1898 Heals published their *Plain Oak Furniture* catalogue. Well known companies including Morris and Company, the Guild of Handicraft, Wylie and Lochhead, Bath Cabinet Makers, Christopher Pratt of Bradford, Norman and Stacey, and J.P. White also produced catalogues which have survived and can be viewed in public archives and library collections.

Catalogues were also promoted from within the trade, and there are many examples of reviews of the latest catalogues in furniture trade journals. *The Furniture Gazette* was very keen to review and promote as the heading to their review in 1891 shows:-

'*New Trade Catalogues. Design Books and Lists*

Catalogues and Price Lists of any and every department in the Furniture Trade should be sent to the Editor immediately they are ready for issue. Mention will then be made of them.'[39]

In the production of a catalogue, a furniture manufacturer would incur significant expense to create the images by drawing or photography and then to pay for design and publishing to a high standard. A good example of the dynamics of catalogue production exists in the record of a legal dispute between Oetzmann and Lefeverer in 1901 in the matter of copying of images in a catalogue. The plaintiff reported that the preparation of their catalogue has cost £8000. This catalogue included 170 pages of illustration and was '*sometimes sold for two shillings and sixpence.*'[40] Within the reporting of the case there was also reference to the production of a sale catalogue for which 250,000 copies were produced at a total cost of £1000 to £1200.

3.4 Catatlogue Shapland and Petter Wood Mantel Pieces. Museum of Barnstaple and North Devon

3.5 Catalogue Shapland and Petter High Class Furniture. Museum of Barnstaple and North Devon

HIGH-CLASS FVRNITVRE

DESIGNS ARRANGED IN THE FOLLOWING ORDER.
EACH SECTION HAVING INDEX IN FRONT.

1. Hall Furniture.
2. Library Furniture, Drawing Room Bookcases and Writing Tables.
3. Wall Cabinets, Smokers' Cupboards, Bookshelves.
4. Drawing Room Cabinets, Music Cabinets, Music Seats.
5. Palm Stands, Cake Stands, Tables, Screens, Mirrors, Overmantels, Coal Boxes, &c.
6. Sideboards.
7. Bedroom Furniture.
8. Wood Bedsteads.

SHAPLAND & PETTER, Ltd. RALEIGH WORKS, BARNSTAPLE.

3.6 Catalogue. Shapland and Petter High Class Furniture.

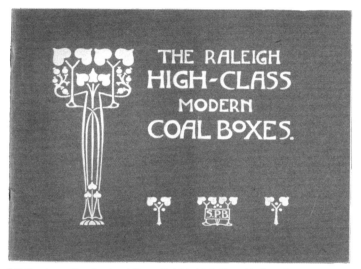

3.7 Catalogue. Shapland and Petter Raleigh High Class Modern Coal Boxes

3.8 Catalogue. Shapland and Petter Wall Cabinets, Smokers Cupboards and Bookshelves

Shapland and Petter Catalogues

When Henry Petter joined with Shapland in about 1854 he brought with him a very important skill. As a publisher he knew the power of the printed word and more so the power of illustration. Petter, the son of a local cooper, born in Barnstaple in about 1827, worked in London for the publishing company Cassell, Petter and Galpin. He severed his connection with the company objecting to the publishing of 'certain books', his religious beliefs causing his decision to withdraw from the firm. When he returned to Barnstaple to become editor of the *North Devon Journal* he met Henry Shapland.

Ernest Shapland writing in the *Cabinet Maker*[41] reported that his father Henry Shapland, took Henry Petter into partnership and he then proved his latent ability as a traveller and became a most successful representative, and opening up business as far north as Inverness in Scotland:-

'Mr Henry Petter took the North of England and Scotland ; Arthur Shapland the Midlands and the South. In London Arthur met Mr Brown, the designer of Newman Street and a catalogue was then produced which was by far the best issued for a furniture firm and is well worth looking at today.'[42]

At the time of writing, no evidence of this early catalogue has been found. However Henry Petter and Arthur Shapland must have used this catalogue to show off the furniture and to win business, taking the firm forward from a provincial cabinet maker to a national supplier with a retail network.

High Class Furniture Photographic Catalogues

In 2004 the author was contacted via his website by a collector who had discovered an original catalogue of Shapland and Petter furniture entitled *High Class Furniture* which was subsequently acquired for the Museum of Barnstaple and North Devon. With confirmation of the title of this catalogue it was then possible to search archives on the title, as previous searches on the name of the company had failed. This research identified another copy (possibly a later version) of this large catalogue and five smaller brochures which consisted of separately bound chapters of the full catalogue. These precious items had eluded previous searches under the company name as the record for them in the catalogue was simply 'S.P-B. Firm' rather than Shapland and Petter or Raleigh.[43]

Evidence of the publication of other catalogues emerged from the large collection of material in the Barnstaple Museum archive and also from the Leaderflush Shapland Company in the form of a fragment of a catalogue on wood mantel pieces and a hard cover of a 'Drawing Room' book but with no content. No details of publisher, or dates of publication exist for any of the catalogues discovered to date, with the one exception of the China Cabinets Catalogue which is dated 1906.

The recently acquired *High Class Furniture* catalogue is divided into sections as shown in the illustration and has over 200 pages showing approximately 600 pieces of furniture and bedroom suites of which approximately one third could be described as in Arts and Crafts style to a greater or lesser extent. Whilst the catalogue seems comprehensive, many items known to exist from photographs in the archives or elsewhere are not shown in the catalogue. There are also some beds and bedroom suites which are illustrated in the separate *Bedroom Furniture* catalogue but not in the large comprehensive version.

Research in the National Art Library indicated that further catalogues must have existed, an article published in 1905 for example, referring to a review of Shapland and Petter's shop in shop in Berners Street mentions that:-

'The firm has just published a booklet entitled Inexpensive Sideboards which contains illustrations and particulars of many other designs and styles. From another of their booklets, "Firescreens" we have selected the other design which adorns this page.'[44]

This illustration, shown 5.23, is not in other catalogues of Shapland and Petter known to date, and offers another tantalising glimpse of the range of Arts and Crafts pieces produced by the firm.

The Catalogue of Drawings

Following the discovery of the *High Class Furniture* catalogues, publicity from the museum in press statements and the author's website appealed for further information on catalogues or marketing materials. In February 2005 Mark Golding contacted the author and Museum with the news that he had discovered a catalogue of drawings relating to Shapland and Petter, and this was subsequently acquired on behalf of the museum.

The catalogue is a compendium of drawings produced and printed as a trade catalogue which displays the range of items available. It has hundreds of drawings including well known pieces, and substantial overlap with items shown in the *High Class Furniture* catalogues. However there are many illustrations of hitherto undocumented pieces such as the hall robe and mirror decorated with peacock inlay and the hall settle shown 3.12. The bookcases shown 6.19 were also a popular line with Shapland and Petter as several are known to exist, but until this catalogue was discovered, no documentation of these pieces was known in any archive material. The catalogue also has examples which appear to be of an earlier style, typical of mid to late Victorian furniture.

3.9 Catalogue. Shapland and Petter Bedroom Furniture

3.10 Catalogue. Shapland and Petter China Cabinets of Artistic Design and High Class Manufacture. 1906

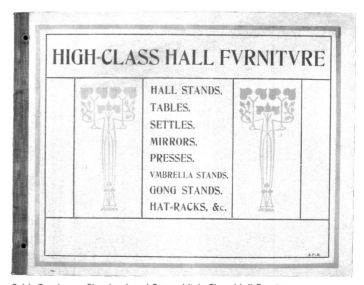

3.11 Catalogue. Shapland and Petter High Class Hall Furniture

3.12 Shapland and Petter. Catalogue of Drawings. Inlaid Hall Furniture. Museum of Barnstaple and North Devon

Catalogues to charm and to inform customers

It is clear from the text beside every item that the catalogues were intended to be used to order bespoke furniture to be made to the customer's specification rather than choose from goods already made and waiting in stock. Many items were described as available in wainscot oak, walnut, or mahogany and where decorated, options for inlaid marquetry, copper panels, or stencilled panels were offered.

It is presumed that some of the more popular items were made as stock and showpieces for Shapland and Petter's main retailers, for local showrooms in Barnstaple and for their own shop in London. Whilst their advertisement in the *Furniture Record* in 1902[45] referred to the fact that there were *"Large Stocks Ready"* this would be to reassure prompt delivery and given the enormous range of possible items which could be required to be in stock, it is much more likely that most pieces would be made to order. The practice of making to order would save waste and appears to have been the practice even in the early years of the

company. Reports of the fire in 1888 mentioned the large stock of completed furniture orders waiting for delivery which were destroyed in the fire.[46]

Within the catalogues, items were numbered and these numbers correspond to the items shown in the company archive of photographs. It is interesting that furniture is shown as individual items, or sets for the hall or library rather than as part of furnished rooms, as was common in the catalogues for Liberty, Wylie and Lochhead, Waring and Gillows and Heals. Only in the case of bedroom suites are pieces shown as part of a room scheme and there are no examples of Shapland and Petter trying to create a 'look' as did Morris and Co, Liberty, Heals and other furnishers. This was perhaps a missed opportunity, but may have had the advantage of increasing the involvement of customers in designing their own furnishing scheme, giving a greater opportunity to exercise taste and creativity.

In the *High Class Furniture* catalogues items are priced, which was significant in that it enabled customers to browse without having to enquire, empowering them as consumers, giving them the ability to choose freely. Whilst we may take price tags for granted today, their introduction in the mid Victorian era marked a break with tradition. Price tags were introduced at the Paris Exposition in 1855 and adventurous shops such as Morris and Co. in Oxford Street used them, at a time when many shops would expect customers to speak to assistants to enquire and possibly negotiate the cost of furniture items.

The practice of making up furniture to the customer's requirement may have been perceived by the customers as giving a greater status to them, allowing them choice rather than accepting what was given. Customers could select, suggest modifications and make 'artistic choices' to ensure the very best results. There are a number of examples of pieces of furniture with variations from the catalogue. There is too, a sense in which customers could commission pieces, rather than just mix and match from the options in the catalogue. Photographs in the archive occasionally have notes added of customers names which suggests involvement in commissioning individual pieces.

Catalogues to enlist retailers to sell products

The importance of the catalogue in marketing cannot be overestimated. Copies left with major retailers could be a low maintenance marketing tool, working for the company to display their wares and attract customers. With their fine catalogues Shapland and Petter would have a presence in the new department stores springing up across the country. The department store, described by Rosalind Williams as *"an environment of mass consumption"*[47] gave consumers the impression of the exotic and the luxurious being available to them. Williams in discussing mass consumption in nineteenth century France talks of the *"dream world"* of the consumer, in which stores and catalogues create an impression of wealth, and focus customers as an audience to be entertained by commodities; images of furniture in catalogues creating *'arousal of free floating desire.'*[48]

It is clear from the Shapland and Petter company records that commercial links were established with dozens of retail furnishers and department stores by the turn of the century. The list shown in Chapter 7 includes names entered in the sales accounts for the company, names written on photographs in the archive and retailers' labels found on items of Shapland and Petter furniture. A printed card for Shapland and Petter in 1912 discovered in archive material at the National Art Library records 30% discount as commission to retailers, which would be a significant incentive.

It is interesting to note the names of a number of major department stores listed in the archive during the late 1890s to early years of 1900 (see figure 1 Chapter 7). Later accounts also show dealings with Harvey Nichols, Aquascutum, and Harrods of London. The archive shows many references to Waring and Gillows, in England and also in Paris and Madrid, in contrast there only three references to Liberty (see Chapter 6). This gives very little support to the widely held belief that Shapland and Petter made many pieces on instructions from Liberty.

One particular marketing technique for furniture manufacturers at the time was to allow their own products to be sold under the name of another company. In the record of the dispute between Oetzmann and Lefeverer, it is mentioned that Messrs Light published a catalogue and offered it to retailers to put their own name on. J.T. Norman were also reported to have printed their catalogues with retailers' names in order for the retailers to distribute as their own. A review in 1901 describes a new catalogue as:-

'Of imposing proportions, and most graphically illustrated by means of drawings the new catalogue of Mr H.L.Benjamin… is pretty sure to find a place in the office of most dealers and house furnishers. As it is arranged the retailer can place it before his customer as practically his own catalogue from which he could supply any desired pattern at the prices named in connection with the admirable drawn designs.'[49]

It appears that Shapland and Petter did not have any inhibitions about allowing other companies to sell Barnstaple products as their own wares. There are several examples in the catalogues of Norman and Stacey, Wylie and Lochhead, and Pratts of Bradford of well known Shapland and Petter Arts and Crafts pieces without attribution. The Wylie and Lochhead catalogue not only has the same pieces but even has the same photographs as used in the Shapland and Petter catalogue for several illustrations e.g. for pieces number 904 and 1541.[50]

Fig 1 Prices of Shapland and Petter Furniture. A comparison.

Catalogue/Price	S&P High Class Furniture circa 1906	Wylie and Lochhead 1902	Norman and Stacey 1902
Smokers Table R904	£5 5s 0d	£4 17s 6d	£4 2s 6d
Hall Seat R1073	£2 12s 6d	£2 10s 0d	£2 12s 6d
Umbrella Stand R1137	£2 7s 6d	£3 15s 0d	£2 7s 6d

3.13 Guild of Handicraft sideboard 1903 Arts and Crafts in Campden. Pg 14

3.14 Advertisement for J.P. White Catalogue. Connoisseur 1902

Competitive Pricing

It is interesting to compare prices between companies for one or two items and Fig 1 shows that pieces in the Shapland and Petter catalogue were a little more expensive than Wylie and Lochhead. This is probably due to the fact that Shapland and Petter prices are for a later period, most likely to be between 4 and 6 years after the other two which were published around 1902.[51]

Shapland and Petter prices compare reasonably with Liberty. The 'Sir Walter Raleigh' oak smokers cabinet with stencilled panel sold for £1 10s 0d at Liberty and a decorated oak cabinet with ornate hinges (R 920) sold at Shapland and Petter for £1 19s; an oak stick stand with pierced hearts sold for £1 7s 6d at Liberty and a similar design (R1422) cost £1 8 s 0d. from Shapland and Petter. Comparing larger items, a mahogany cabinet with 3 inlaid panels 'suitable for a boudoir' sold at Liberty for

£15 10 s 0d and roughly similar cabinets were on sale at Shapland and Petter from £13 to £16 or £20 for more elaborate pieces (R2032,R2032, R2036).

Interesting also to compare prices with Baillie Scott designed furniture at J.P.White. Their 1901 catalogue[52] priced the Daffodil Dresser, with inlaid design in oak at £19 10s. Alternatively, shoppers could go for the Liberty Milverton sideboard at £21 10s. The Shapland and Petter sideboard (R2150) with copper panels as illustrated in *Studio Yearbook 1906*[53] would cost £21 15s in their catalogue. The Guild of Handicraft sideboard in fumed oak with bright steel fittings was a little more expensive at £25. The oak settle for JP White designed by Baillie Scott cost £12 for 5 foot 6 inch. A similar oak settle with inlay model 1090, measuring 4 foot 6 inches cost £9 7s 6d from Shapland and Petter. See 6.14.

3.15 Norman and Stacey Advertisement. Connoisseur. 1903

Affordable Luxury?

To put prices into context its worth considering that cabinet makers would earn around 9 old pence per hour for a 51 hour week in 1901 and their gross pay per week would be approximately £1 18s 3d. So, the pieces they made were very costly in comparison with their own earnings and the more elaborate pieces e.g. the Glasgow rose display cabinet illustrated which cost £30 would have represented several months pay for the men who made it. See 3.18.

Travelling Salesmen

For catalogues to be a successful marketing tool, special efforts were needed to develop and sustain the retail networks required to sell to the public. Travelling salesman or travellers were employed to visit shops and suppliers to persuade them to hold a catalogue from which to encourage customers to choose

904.—SMOKER'S TABLE.

904 Open,
Showing Fittings of Table.

Extreme Height 2 ft. 6 ins.
Top 2 ft. x 1 ft. 4 ins.

Wainscot Oak or Walnut **£5** : 5 : 0

Mahogany ... ... **5** : 10 : 0

With Hammered Copper Top.

3.16 Smokers table R904. High Class Furniture

1073
3 ft. 6 extreme. With Glove Box.
Registered No. 357729.
Wainscot Oak ... ... £2 : 12 : 6
Walnut or Mahogany ... ... 2 : 17 : 6
Copper Drip Pan.

1137
1 ft. 6 x 1 ft. 2.
Wainscot Oak ... ... £2 : 7 : 6
Walnut or Mahogany ... ... 2 : 10 : 0
With Hand Worked Copper or Carved Panel.

3.17 Hall seat R 1073 and Umbrella stand R1137 High Class Furniture

their wares. Travellers did appear to have an important status in the trade at the turn of the century. For example the *Furniture Record* regularly included articles on 'Popular Travellers' and in 1901 featured Mr John Reid, a time served cabinet maker, who is pictured in silk top hat, suit and wing collar with a walking stick. He appears very much the gentleman and ambassador, presumably most effective at winning respect and new business for the company he represented.

'Mr Reid has travelled England Scotland and Ireland, North and South Wales and always met with the greatest kindness from all his customers. His success he attributes… to the practical and thorough training he received as a salesperson and to his love of the work. It is permissible for us to add another factor which has, undoubtedly, had no small share in Mr Reid's success, and that is his personality - gentle character that inspires confidence and unaffected geniality that makes friends.' [54]

We know that Henry Petter also was particularly good at this task of travelling, and before him, in the early days of the business, Henry Shapland was introduced to a tea traveller from London, who sold his early wavy mouldings to piano manufacturers in the city at a commission of 25%. This was not a long-standing arrangement, as Henry's son Ernest recorded:

'After a while it occurred to my father that this was a high rate of remuneration, so he thanked the traveller and told him he had decided to sell his mouldings himself and thus ended their successful business connection.' [55]

It is fairly clear that the status of travellers was high and they were required to be extremely knowledgeable about the business of making furniture. Henry's son Richard Arthur Shapland had been:-

'apprenticed at the bench and was considered a very skilled young workman and was deemed by my father to be capable of becoming a traveller, and off he was sent to London.' [56]

Another son, Ernest was also travelling on behalf of the firm at that time, making many trips abroad presumably to generate business and link with existing customers in Spain, France and further afield.

Travellers' wages were recorded in the ledgers and an entry for 1898 shows the amount of £954 10s paid for travellers' and agents' wages but it is not clear how many were on the staff at this time. The ledger for 1908 records that W.J. Ponter was appointed traveller for the Midlands, to be paid £150 p.a. plus £150 expenses guaranteed for the first year, with 5% commission if orders exceeded £6,000 p.a. There are also records of incidental payments as commission for sales won by senior designer William Cowie and others.

The Shop at Berners Street in London

During the latter part of the nineteenth century Shapland and Petter developed a very effective commercial organisation to sell the company products and their sales network clearly brought them business. Whilst they could have continued to develop selling through provincial retailers a decision was made to establish a shop, right in the heart of London's West End in Berners Street. This was to be their flagship and their presence amongst the top furnishers and department stores in the country at the time.

Company records show Shapland and Petter paying rent for Berners Street from 1893 onwards and an article in a contemporary journal mentions their showrooms:-

'Their showrooms at number 67 Berners Street every week contain some 'new thing of beauty', either in sideboards, bedroom suites 'artistic joinery' &c which should be seen by all houses who wish to have their stock as the newest style and design. Just now the firm are showing some delightful specimens of Empire Bedroom suits in mahogany and light woods with ormolu mounts which are exceedingly choice and effective. Buyers where possible should visit the works.' [57]

3.18 Mahogany display cabinet
with inlaid design. R2027

2027
Extreme Height 6 ft. 7 in.; Extreme Width 4 ft. 6 in.
Convex Panes in Centre Doors. Cupboard Lined Plush or Silk Tapestry.
2 Polished Plate Glass Shelves. Bevelled Mirrors in Back.
Mahogany Inlaid with Pearl and } £30 : 0 : 0
     Coloured Woods ... ... }
Sheraton treatment (Satinwood Bandings, etc.) 28 : 10 : 0

652   THE FURNITURE RECORD AND THE FURNISHER.   JUNE 24 1904

SHAPLAND & PETTER, Ltd.,

Raleigh Cabinet Works,

Telegrams: "Raleigh, Barnstaple."   Telephone: No. 9.   **BARNSTAPLE.**

MANUFACTURERS AND EXPORTERS OF

High Class Furniture of Original Character.

Interior of London Showrooms at

61, BERNERS STREET, OXFORD STREET, W.

Telegrams: "Shapland, Berners Street, London."   Telephone: 4324 Central.

Suggestions and Estimates for Fitments and Interior Woodwork of every description.

MANTELPIECES, PANELLING, Etc.

3.19 Shapland and Petter. Advertisement. Furniture Record. June 1904

Presumably this advertisement was directed at the furniture trade, 'houses' referring to furnishers, and buyers in the trade, but it appears that they extended their business and showrooms making them accessible for the public. An observer writing in Barnstaple, in 1897 commented that:-

'The factory has been considerably extended during the past two or three years. Last year spacious showrooms were opened in Berners Street, London so that the business is now well represented in the metropolis.'[58]

By 1902 Shapland and Petter took a full page in a contemporary journal advertising their Berners Street offices and showrooms. Strategically, setting up shop in Berners Street was very shrewd. Economically it completed the chain of processes from buying trees, to cutting and drying timber, to making furniture, and then selling directly to the customer with no discounts to pay to other retailers. The importance of having a London shop was recognised by a number of furniture companies, including those which specialised in Arts and Crafts.

In 1875 Authur Lazenby Liberty opened his shop in Regent Street and in 1887 William Morris opened his own shop in Oxford Street, not far from Liberty. In an appraisal of William Morris business techniques, Harvey and Press[59] emphasise that while Morris and Co may have looked to the past for technique and inspiration, in business Morris himself was very modern in his approach and knew how to get the attention of possible customers. The shop in Oxford Street was 'the strategic hub' of the business where goods were displayed tastefully in a fashionable setting and the commercial managers based there drew very high salaries in recognition of their important functions.

In 1908 Shapland and Petter recruited Mr Wade formerly of Hamptons, to be the 'designer' at the Berners Street shop, with his duties to attend to customers and a salary of £2 10s per week plus 2 weeks paid holiday he would certainly be a cut above the average shop assistant. Presumably the title of designer was intended to convey that he would engage with customers and advise them on the selection of furniture to help them create an artistic and thoughtful scheme of design. The head of the shop was Robert Yenke or 'Mr Jenks' often referred to in reviews of the shop as 'their London representative, and known for his 'courteous guidance'. In 1905 it was reported in a review that:-

'It is not possible to exhibit in the London showrooms specimens of all designs but Mr Jenks has a complete representation of the productions of the Barnstaple factory and is therefore in a position to satisfy the requirements of the most exigent of buyers.'[60]

London was the capital of the furniture trade at the turn of the century with a concentration of cabinet makers sweatshops and manufacturers in and around the centre. A number of companies which specialised in Arts and Crafts styles were in walking distance of each other. Morris and Co were on Oxford Street, near to Shapland and Petter at 61 Berners Street, Bath Cabinet Makers at Number 5, and Walter Skull at 45 Berners Street. The mighty Liberty were in Regent Street and almost next door J.P. White in Margaret Street. From here it was a short walk to Bond Street, to the Guild of Handicraft at Derring Yard, 67a Bond Street, and 17a Brook Street. Also in New Bond Street were George Wardle and W.A.S Benson selling art metalwork. Further afield, we find J.S. Henry at 287/291 Old Street, Heals in Tottenham Court Road, and Norman and Stacey at 118 Queen Victoria Street.

Given the proximity of these shops it would be quite easy to keep an eye on each others latest designs. Their closeness, in such a prestigious part of London may also have brought benefit in terms of suggesting to customers that these shops were part of a coherent style with depth and breadth.

3.20 Goodyers Advertisement. Connoisseur 1903

In their location in Berners Street, Shapland and Petter were surrounded by 'artistic' and fashionable shops with a distinct emphasis on decorative arts. Bath Cabinet Makers further along the Street would also be showing their highly decorated furniture. Other interesting shops would include at number 64, Alfred Newey Art Metal Worker working in Arts and Crafts style and at number 9, Cloisonné Glass. Nearby were John Line and Sons Decorators and Arthur Dix stained glass makers.

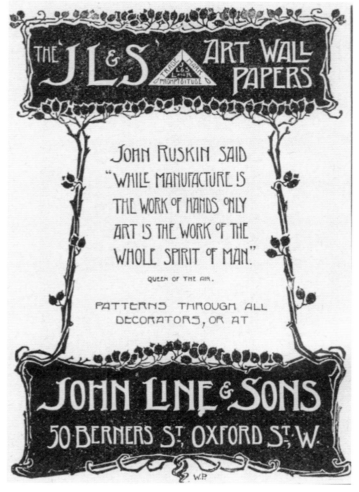

3.21 John Line, Berners Street. The Studio Vol 21 1900

3.22 Arthur Dix, Berners Street. The Studio Vol 21 1900

Advertising and Reviews;

Use of photography

Within the *High Class Furniture* Catalogues discovered to date, furniture is illustrated predominantly by photographs of pieces against neutral backgrounds, with occasional use of line drawings and watercolour drawings reproduced in black and white. Photography was the main media used, and within the records of Shapland and Petter there are costs shown for photography and a single reference to payment for watercolours by Miss C Shapland. In 1900 a payment of £24 was recorded, and also *'Photographic Purchases lens and plates from Abbott and Son.'* In 1902 the ledger records purchase of a *'Photographic studio for fifty pounds twelve shillings and sixpence'*, with a further purchase of eighteen pounds for photographic items. Clearly, by this time the company realised the importance of photography in marketing and had developed their own studio. It is very typical of their business style to develop their own 'in house' studio rather than pay for an outside contractor. As well as saving on costs, their own studio also gave them the opportunity to develop consistency in background and the use of a little stock of vases (including Barnstaple Art Pottery and Minton's Art Nouveau), books and umbrellas to adorn the items displayed. Photographs

Fig. 4.—A fine and dignified example of modern æsthetic art. It is white, with deep blue curtains and marquetry panels. A specimen of good taste.

3.23 Shapland and Petter wardrobe. White with inlaid Glasgow roses. Furniture Record Oct 1905

3.24 Inlaid panel of Glasgow roses for wardrobe shown 3.23

3.25 Shapland and Petter review. Furniture Record Sept 1903

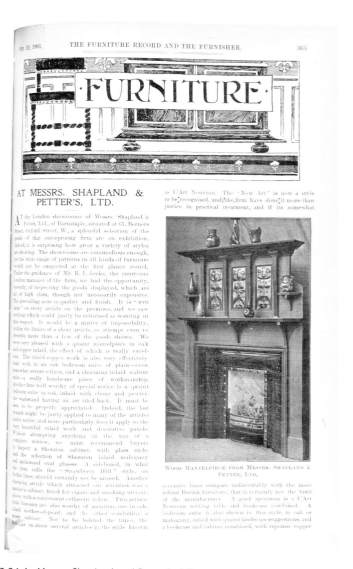

3.26 At Messrs Shapland and Petter Ltd. Furniture Record Oct 1901

were also used to keep a record of all items produced and the archive contains thousands of images with design numbers and other information on size, retailers and other occasional detail.

Having photographs of their products strengthened their marketing strategy through advertising and there are several examples in the ledgers of costs for placing adverts in local periodicals between 1896 and 1902 which include the *Bideford Gazette, Western Morning News, South West Guide, Cornishman*, and the *Royal Cornwall Gazette*. Advertisements were also placed in national periodicals for the trade such as *British Architect, Cabinet Maker, Kelly's Directory, Ironmongers Chronicle, Furniture and Decoration*, Costs of between £6 and £9 were recorded for these. The annual cost of advertising varied from about £30 to £50 per year, so not a very great outlay in relative terms. Four full page advertisements have been discovered to date and these are illustrated. See 1.1, 1.16, 2.3, 3.19.

Reviews in Trade Journals

An important source of publicity for companies like Shapland and Petter was to receive a review in trade journals and there are several examples of Shapland and Petter promotional reviews. It is probably no coincidence that Shapland and Petter adverts also appear in issues of reviewing journals and presumably this was a negotiated arrangement, very much as one might expect today, i.e. a positive review of products is given provided advertising is purchased.

We can glean quite a lot about the image of Shapland and Petter from these reviews. In the main, reviews praised the company for achieving the highest class designs and construction using the very latest technology and in the most up to the minute artistic style. Whilst they were producing a range of styles of furniture at the time of the reviews, it is the Arts and Crafts pieces which are featured very often with the label of 'artistic'.

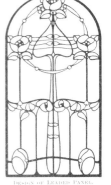

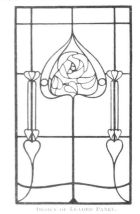

British Exhibition at Buda=Pesth.

3.27 Budapest Exhibition. Furniture Record. Nov 1902 pg 547

3.28 Budapest Exhibition. Furniture Record. Nov 1902 pg 548

Sketches from West End windows

A particularly interesting feature which ran through several editions of the *Furniture Record* in 1905 was 'Notes and sketches for the retailer'. Examples of furniture on show in shop windows in the West End of London were selected and sketched by a 'rambling' reporter who then gave each item a write up in his column. Whilst the usual practice was not to disclose names of individual manufacturers.

Quaint and Chaste

Several items shown in sketches appear to be Shapland and Petter pieces and one in particular stands out, the wardrobe illustrated 3.23. The description says:-

'Here we have a serviceable wardrobe (save that there is a total absence of a mirror). It is white and is decorated with bold copper hinges and handles. The curtains in the top recesses are blue silk, not

the mawkish neutral tints of 'Patience' days and the panels of the doors are decorated with strongly coloured and strong drawn marquetry on a deep blue ground. The lines and the mouldings are firmly designed and the general appearance of the whole of the suite denotes strenuous good taste.'[61]

Budapest Exhibition 1902

It is clear that in the furniture business, exhibitions were a very powerful way of bringing products to customers, before the days of mass advertising. The Arts and Crafts Exhibitions which started in 1888, carried on the tradition of earlier events which followed on from the 1851 exhibition. The Art Applied to Furniture Exhibition in 1881 and also the first Furniture Trades Exhibition were followed by others in Manchester, Liverpool and then those of the Arts and Crafts Society held in London in 1888, 1889, 1890 and every 3 years after that.

By the 1890's reviews of exhibitions were regularly published in *The Studio, The Cabinet Maker, The Artist, Architect* and similar periodicals, providing excellent free publicity for companies and helping to influence taste by introducing the Arts and Crafts style. Articles included reports of the Arts and Crafts Exhibitions in major cities and in London, with photographs of furniture, metalwork and other items.

Major events in the world of furniture and design included the Glasgow Exhibition in 1901 at which Glasgow School designers broke through from relative obscurity to notoriety and then glowing acclaim in *The Studio* and other periodicals. Further afield the Paris Exposition in 1900 had attracted exhibitors from Britain, which included furniture from Ambrose Heal and J.S. Henry, and the Turin Exhibition at which Charles Rennie Mackintosh and other Glasgow School designers won acclaim in 1902.

There is no mention of Shapland and Petter in the reports of any exhibition until the exhibition in Budapest in 1902 when a feature article gave prominent position to their exhibit. The catalogue for the exhibition was designed by Glasgow designer George Walton, and the Glasgow firms of Wylie and Lochhead, and Guthrie and Wells (who made furniture for Charles Rennie Mackintosh) were represented. Other firms included Edgar Wood of Manchester and the Bath Cabinet Makers.

In a review of the exhibition, Shapland and Petter were singled out for special mention and their pieces of furniture are the only furniture illustrated.

'We give a few illustrations of some notable exhibits foremost among which must be placed the goods of Messrs Shapland and Petter Ltd... The high class productions of this firm are too well known to the best houses of this country to need much introduction. With such worthy representatives of British art furniture we may feel quite satisfied that our prestige is being maintained.'[63]

Protecting designs through Registration

One further strategy which was employed to secure and develop business was to register company designs. Registering designs was a strategy to protect 'piracy' or the copying of designs and though some furniture manufacturers such as Lebus used this frequently, others like Shapland and Petter seemed to have employed it very rarely. Whilst many Shapland and Petter pieces have numbers stamped into the wood on the back of the piece these numbers do not signify registered designs. These stamped numbers are discussed further in Chapter 7.

One company, which appeared to have made very determined efforts to prevent piracy was Liberty and their records in the Westminster Archive contains two large files of correspondence on 'Piracies' from the late nineteenth and early twentieth century. A number of these relate to companies using the word Liberty to describe materials but there are also instances where furniture designs are involved. In one example, Arts and Crafts furniture designer J.S. Henry writes to defend himself against an alleged attempt to copy and publish Liberty designs.[64]

Shapland and Petter did seem more relaxed in their approach to registration. The National Archive Register of Designs records six S&P applications between 1884-94. Though there are several entries in the Shapland and Petter cash book around 1900 to 1902 for Registration of designs (cost 6 shillings), to date only two pieces of furniture produced by Shapland and Petter have been found to bear registration numbers, the hall seat illustrated 3.29 and a Music Cabinet. The hall seat bears an ivorine label with registration number (see Chapter 7) and was identified in the Register of designs by the author, in 2004. The registration number for the music cabinet could not be linked to other than a blank entry in the register for that year. Presumably both items were registered because they included some innovative design i.e. the attachment of a glove box which gave sufficient novelty to warrant taking out a patent to protect from competition.

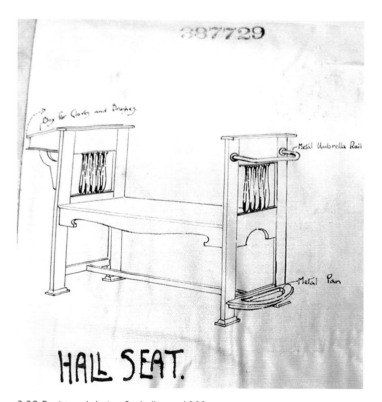

3.29 Registered design for hall seat 1902

3.30 Mahogany hallstand with copper panel. R1058

Chapter 4 Decoration and Design

4.1 Tile from Shapland and Petter hallstand

This chapter looks at the themes and motifs which characterise the decoration of Arts and Crafts furniture made by Shapland and Petter.

Sources of Inspiration; Fantasy and Myths and Legends

Much of the imagery in decoration used by Arts and Crafts designers has a medieaval theme which reflects the richly coloured and romantic world depicted by Pre-Raphaelite painters. The Pre-Raphaelite Brotherhood was formed in 1848 and this group of seven painters took classical and religious scenes for their subjects but also created scenes of medieaval and legendary figures such as King Arthur and St George. Seeking truth to nature and 'archaic honesty' in their work they painted in bright colours with intensity of feeling.

In the 1850's and 60's Rossetti, Ford Maddox Brown and Burne-Jones created images of medieaval, Arthurian and literary characters with ladies and knights in armour painted in dramatic and romantic poses. These images in pictures, painted panels, tapestries, embroidery and stained glass established the powerful tradition for historical and romantic themes in visual and decorative arts which lasted through till the end of the century.

The fascination with the legend of King Arthur and scenes of Guinevere and Camelot were a recurring theme throughout the Arts and Crafts movement. In 1858 William Morris's poem *In Defence of Guinevere* was published and even before this Rossetti had begun to include Arthurian legend and ballad images in his work. 40 years later, Shapland and Petter were still including images of knights and maidens in their stencilled and painted panels and the rare tile illustrated 4.1.[65]

Whilst Pre-Raphaelite imagery was a vital influence on the artistic development of the Arts and Crafts movement in the early years of the Victorian era, it was so for only a small group of serious thinkers engaged in decorative design. However, by the end of the nineteenth century their popularity had grown. Popular journals such as *The Studio*, and *The Artist* around the turn of the century are replete with images of maidens in fairytale castles, with illustrated nursery rhymes, scenes from Shakespeare, Chaucer and Robin Hood illustrated in swirling and romantic style. Shapland and Petter drew upon these popular images and some examples survive of their painted work, for example the Canterbury Tales bookshelf illustrated 4.5.

Ships and Boats

Another popular theme in Arts and Crafts design was of ships, often in the Viking longboat style or the galleon with billowing sail. The sailing ship was a popular image for art potters and for metalworkers, particularly John Pearson and craftsmen in the Newlyn School of Industrial Art in Cornwall at the turn of the century, and was also an emblem for the Guild of Handicrafts. It is said that sailing ships symbolise a voyage of intellectual discovery and as such were a fitting emblem for the progressive and creative Arts and Crafts movement.

4.2 Stencilled panel from oak overnmantel. R6017

4.3 Hall cupboard with stencilled panels. R1085. Photo archive

Shapland and Petter used sailing ship designs in painted panels for a buffet, an overmantle, and smokers cabinets, in stained glass for a firescreen and in repoussé copper for firescreens, hall settles and smaller items. A description of one copper panel in a settle in the catalogue of drawings is of a 'galley'.

Figures and portraits

Decorative pieces by Shapland and Petter included rather superficial pieces with stencilled and painted design of a gentleman in eighteenth century dress with cocked hat and lace cuffs pictured smoking or taking snuff. Similar designs were shown on smoking cabinets retailed by Liberty. Other more attractive pieces show the faces of women in Pre-Raphaelite pose. The cabinet illustrated 5.30 is a rare survivor of what may have been a popular line for the company. The tile was designed by later pre Raphaelite painter and illustrator, Eleanor Fortescue Brickdale whose work was frequently shown in *The Studio*, depicting heroic scenes often with inscriptions. The tile is entitled Chance.[66]

A striking image of a young woman in a stylised landscape was stencilled and painted on bookcases and on beds shown in the archive, overmantles and, possibly on other items. Another image used was that of a young woman in a landscape with windmill. See 4.7 to 4.11.

Landscapes

Stencilled and inlaid pictures of landscapes were also used to great effect. The panels illustrated 4.14 showing sunrise and sunset on a wooded landscape were used for hall robes, the overmantle mirror shown and possibly other items. Similar but distinctly different landscape designs were stencilled and painted on furniture retailed by Liberty, the Athelstan suite in particular. The landscape with stream and irises and cottage in the

4.4 Wall mounted magazine rack with copper panel R2454. Photo archive

background shows a rural idyll and seems only to have been used for the bureau bookcase illustrated 4.13. A very high quality decorative design was that of the village scene portrayed in inlaid woods, and this appears only to have been used on the oak bureau illustrated 2.1. This piece came in several similar versions in oak and mahogany. Other designs employed, particularly in stencilled and painted form, included chickens, a bowman and a scene of horsemen and hounds.

Dutch Scenes

Holland seemed to be a very popular venue for artistic pursuits at the turn of the century and *The Studio* had fairly frequent references to painting and drawing in Dutch and Belgian towns. Cartoon versions of these scenes, windmills and barges seemed to be eagerly adopted by commercial producers of Arts and Crafts 'Novelties', Liberty featured several items with these themes in their *Yuletide Gifts* Catalogues around the turn of the century. Shapland and Petter clearly wanted to be included on this particular bandwagon and the smokers cabinet 4.15 includes a large tile with Dutch theme. This tile was also used on a tray. A single photograph found within the archive shows a room decorated with a frieze with stylised Dutch figures in a landscape and including an oak sideboard with inset panels 4.16.

4. 6 Oak smokers cabinet with painted galleon. R920

4.7 Detail stencilled panel

4.8 Detail overmantel panel. R6018

4.5 Oak bookshelf with stencilled panel. R861

6018.

3 ft. 2 wide on base; 2 ft. 4 high.

With Stencilled Panel and Translucent Enamels on Copper.

Enamelled Ivory White	...	...	...	...	£3 : 11 : 6
Wainscot Oak	...	...	...	...	3 : 11 : 6
Walnut or Mahogany	...	...	...	...	3 : 15 : 0

4.9 High Class Furniture; overmantels

4.10 Oak bookcase with stencilled panel.

6027.

4 ft. 6 wide ; 2 ft. 10 high.

Enamelled Ivory White	...	...	...	£6 : 0 : 0
Wainscot Oak	...	...	...	6 : 0 : 0
Mahogany	...	...	...	6 : 7 : 6

With Stencilled Panel and Translucent Enamels on Copper.

4.11 High Class Furniture; overmantels

Inspiration from the natural world

The decorative style which most people will recognise as Shapland and Petter is that which shows plant forms stylised and in matrix like shapes contained within panels. Whilst a range of plant forms were used, it is the roses, the lilies, poppies, honesty and bursting seedpods that have given Shapland and Petter pieces their distinctive character. Before we consider these, there are first of all the birds and the beasts to deal with.

Peacocks, Doves and Swallows

The representation of the peacock was common in Arts and Crafts design and was said to be the epitome of the Aesthetic movement before it. This bird was the pagan symbol of immortality and Christian symbol of the Resurrection. The inlaid peacock pattern was commonly used by Shapland and Petter for their finer pieces such as display cabinets, firescreens and hall cupboards either in mahogany or oak. The hall robe and mirror illustrated are good examples and the archive photographs show a fine firescreen, fire surround and display cabinets in the same pattern. See for example 6.4.

The best known peacock design is probably that of the feather designed by Arthur Silver and manufactured for Liberty from 1887. Several Shapland and Petter designs seem very similar to this fabric, being based on feathers or a stylised form similar to a nut kernel or seedpod.

Other birds were also represented in Arts and Crafts design, Charles Rennie Mackintosh, Voysey and Baillie Scott frequently used images of swallows or similar birds in flight, and of doves either in stained glass or as inlaid design. The dove was a symbol of the Holy Ghost in the religious sense, and in the secular sense a symbol of innocence, affection and constancy. Shapland and Petter depicted pairs of doves in inlaid design, and in repoussé copper, similar to Baillie Scott designs. The hall cupboard shown 4.20 was a very popular line and several examples of this piece are known to exist in private collections.

Shapland and Petter designs also included an owl, symbol of wisdom, in repoussé copper on a stick stand, a pelican, symbol of redemption and resurrection, depicted in a small copper roundel inset in a hanging cabinet, and a stork or heron depicted in repoussé and chased copper panels on a hall stand. Another interesting pattern included in an elaborately decorated hall cupboard is of a mythical beast, possibly a lion, similar to designs created by Voysey. See 6.27. The Catalogue of Drawings includes bedroom furniture decorated with inlaid designs of fish and birds in carved mother of pearl but these appear not to be in Arts and Crafts style.

4.12 Oak magazine rack with stencilled panel. R2454

4.13 Oak bureau bookcase with stencilled panel and inset enamelled heart. R1541

4.14. Oak overmantel with stencilled panels. R 6017

4.15 Oak smokers cabinet with ceramic panel. R863

More rare are the highly decorative pieces such as the inlaid wardrobe which depicts swallows in the design and the hall robe which shows the most elaborate and skillfully depicted scenes of a rider and animals in a wooded landscape 4.19,5.52. This most richly decorated piece is inlaid with the same style of the village scene on the bureau illustrated 2.1. The highest level of skill is evident in this masterpiece of intarsia work. The visual style seems more continental than traditionally English, with Flemish or German influence and is possibly the work of William Deubler, Shapland's freelance inlayer, of whom more in Chapters 5 and 6.

4.16 Photo archive picture; room interior in Dutch style.
Date and origin unknown

Flower and Plant forms

A wide range of floral and plant forms was used in Shapland and Petter designs, most commonly in repoussé copper ornament or inlaid design. The range of designs which have been observed to be used on Shapland and Petter pieces shown in the table in the endnotes.[67]

In most designs, plant forms appear but not as exact representations of individual plant species. A very popular motif was the seedpod bursting to reveal seeds within and offering an image of potency, regeneration and dynamic growth. The image of a bursting seedpod was used by Voysey several years before it appeared in the Shapland and Petter vocabulary. A design for a lady's work cabinet by him, exhibited in the Arts and Crafts Exhibition of 1893 shows a large hinge with central motif of a bursting seedpod and seeds exposed. See 4.23.[68] This symbol of the bursting seedpod was used repeatedly in a variety of forms by Shapland and Petter, most of which bear a similarity to the lotus or water lily flowers, buds and fruit.

Form and rhythm

Floral and organic forms were rarely allowed to scroll in Greek fashion, or stray across furniture and were most often contained within defined panels of rectangular or arched shape. Within the panel the forms tended towards a heraldic and upright flat decoration in a matrix or branched shape of three or five vertical stems, resembling a toasting fork. The patterns were often constructed in three flowers or buds and two intertwining leaves or stems which rose up in an elegant and symmetrical curvaceous form. Five vertical stems or leaves seems to be a recurrent theme in the floral designs and it is common to see a triangular shape or hierarchical form as one bud or flower at the pinnacle of the design with two or four others below as a lower tier.

It is also common to see circular decoration impressed in floral designs in copper from the reverse almost like large full stops or the bubbles in Newlyn copper work depicting fish and marine life. The function of these circles within the Shapland and Petter design appears to emphasise the rhythm of the pattern and they frequently occurred in even numbers either twos, or fours or sixes to contrast the odd numbers of fives and threes in plant form design.

4.17 Mahogany hall mirror peacock feather design. R1406

4.18 Mahogany hall cupboard with inlaid peacocks. R1399

4.19 Oak wardrobe with inlaid panel. R126

4.22 *Oak hanging shelves with inset silvered copper panel. R928*

4.20 *Oak hall cupboard with panel of doves. R1176*

1173

2 ft. 3 on Standards; 3 ft. extreme.
Inlaid.

Wainscot Oak	...	£4 : 10 : 0
Mahogany	...	4 : 15 : 0
Plain.		
Wainscot Oak	...	4 : 7 : 6
Walnut or Mahogany	...	4 : 10 : 0

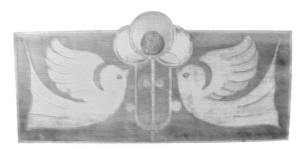

4.21 *Inlaid panel of oak hall stand R1173*

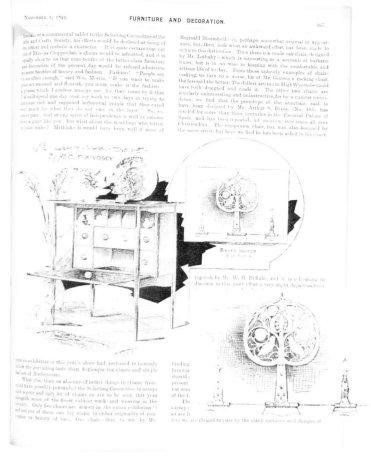

4.23 C.F.A.Voysey Design for a Lady's Work Cabinet. Furniture and Decoration & The Furniture Gazette. 1893

4.24 Shapland and Petter Firescreens; photo archive

4.25 Oak hall mirror with copper panel of thistle design and 'bubbles'. R1410

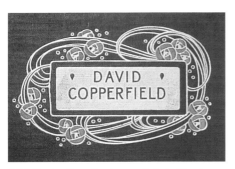

4.26 Design for a book cover. Talwin Morris

4.27 White bedroom suite with copper panels of Glasgow roses. R 214 and detail of panel before restoration.

*4.28 Mahogany display cabinet
inlaid lily design*

4.29 Oak fire surround with inset copper panels. R157

4.30 Oak bookcase with copper panel. R1464

4.31 Oak smoker's cabinet with copper panel and split bud motif. R853

Glasgow rose design

A design which is popular with collectors and has a wide appeal is that of the Glasgow rose. This emanated from the 'School of Four' in Glasgow led by Charles Rennie Mackintosh and was used freely in designs by other members of the Glasgow School in metalwork, furniture decoration, illustration, embroidery, book binding and other decorative arts. The earliest appearance of this design is hard to trace but the stylised roses of the Glasgow School designs were included in items shown in the Arts and Crafts Exhibition in London in 1896 and reviewed in *The Studio* magazine.[69]

A particular application of this style of decoration developed by Glasgow designer Talwin Morris shows the Glasgow rose in a matrix with vertical stems very similar to the pattern widely used by Shapland and Petter. Designs for metalwork featuring Glasgow rose and leaf, by Talwin Morris, were published in *The Studio*.[70]

Shapland and Petter may also have become aware of this design through their contacts with the firm of Wylie and Lochhead who manufactured designs by Glasgow School designers and also bought in furniture from Shapland and Petter. It not clear when Shapland and Petter first started to use the Glasgow rose design but the first public appearance seems to have been in an article about the company published in 1903 which featured photographs of an overmantle and fire surround with inlaid roses in Glasgow Style.[71] See 5.22.

A very striking application of the Glasgow rose design is the incorporation of panels into white painted furniture which in itself reflects the Glasgow School, particularly Mackintosh painted furniture. The application of copper panels or inlaying of coloured woods gives these pieces a very powerful and charismatic appeal.

The Lily, Lotus and Water Lily

The most spectacular use of the lily design is the display cabinet in mahogany which is shown in the illustration 4.28 and this appears to have been a popular line for the company retailed through Berners Street and also through Christopher Pratts of Bradford who feature it in their catalogue. The white lily was seen in Victorian times as a symbol of purity and chastity, and was used particularly by Baillie Scott and others.[72]

Lily buds in various styles are frequently depicted in repoussé copper panels, often in a square box like shape alongside open flower buds, showing seeds or stamens within. From the perspective of a botanist these stylised flowers appear to derive more from the nymphaecea family of the lotus plant and related water lily than the lily Lilium candidum. The pods and fruiting forms shown bear some resemblance to the bottle like fruits of the lotus and water lily and patterns of floating leaves shown in

the silvered hinges on the doors of the mahogany display cabinet illustrated 5.14.

The religious and symbolic significance of the lotus and water lily is said to be linked to the flower opening at dawn and closing at night, symbolising death and renewal, passing into darkness and awakening into new life. This symbolism in Christian terms would relate to the resurrection and the belief in life after death and may have held some importance for Shapland and Petter designer William Cowie known to be Plymouth Brethren.

One feature of the depiction of buds which is interesting is the split which crosses the bud in a yin yang pattern. This is not true to nature as the buds would split vertically rather than spirally across the circumference of the bud. This is a stylisation which has a very satisfying decorative effect, but is in not clear whether it is intended to convey any symbolic significance.

Tulips and Daffodils

Tulips in bud and in open form were frequently depicted in Arts and Crafts decoration. Baillie Scott's published designs in stained glass, in a design for a piano published in *The Studio*[73] and designs for J.P. White furniture[74] are the perhaps the most exuberant use of the design, often with swallows incorporated into the pattern. Shapland and Petter created a number of designs for repoussé copper which show stylised tulips with closed buds or inverted heart shapes interlaced with leaves in a matrix. There are also several variations in this design with semi open flowers showing stamens. These forms are also considered to be very similar to lotus buds.

Daffodils, did not appear to be used widely as a design. Newlyn Copper work which was sold in the South West and in London, featured daffodils in design but it was Baillie Scott who used this design to best effect. His Daffodil Dresser illustrated in the J.P. White Catalogue appears to have inspired many versions. Shapland and Petter produced their own version but it appears to have been rarely used, the small cabinet illustrated in their catalogue being the only example identified to date. See 6.11.

Other plants and trees

There are many further examples of plant forms used in Shapland and Petter decoration which may well be worth examining to establish their origins in nature. Tree forms were used occasionally, two examples being the fruiting trees shown in the copper panel with doves and carved panels of hall robes Illustrated 4.20 and 5.40, and in the particularly beautiful tiles from the Medmenham pottery[75] used in the small wall cabinet illustrated 5.28. Tree of life designs with roots, branches and fruit were popular in Arts and Crafts work, and Shapland and Petter inlaid designs often include berries and fruit.

4.32 Mahogany bookcase with copper panel and inscription. R1464

The Motto or inscription

The use of the mottoes, in the form of lettering applied to furniture, was a popular decorative device. Mottoes usually provide an uplifting word of advice, a quote from literature, or truism and were used by the Arts and Crafts designers Morris, Pugin, Burges, Talbot and Eastlake among many others. Before them, the tradition of applied inscriptions to works of art, as part of the art is evident in medieaval and religious painting, stained glass, tapestry and other decorative artefacts

By the end of nineteenth century mottoes had become almost a cliché of artistic design. Drawings and finished work published or exhibited by Baillie Scott, Voysey and Glasgow School artists featured inscriptions or the 'Bon Mot' before the end of the nineteenth century. By the turn of the century furniture sold by Liberty's, Heals, and Shapland and Petter often featured carved, or stencilled and painted mottoes and there are many examples particularly of Shapland and Petter furniture with mottoes created by repoussé copper panels. See Fig 1.

These companies used mottoes with some measure of restraint but more generally, manufacturers of Arts and Crafts furniture were quick to exploit the commercial value of mottoes and this provoked some criticism. An article on techniques of the 'New Art' in *The Artist* was most sarcastic about the trend:-

'A favourite plan is to introduce a design involving in sweet serpentine sinuosity some appropriate motto text ,wise saw or proverb for this adds grace and finish to porch, fireplace or bedstead etc. ...On a fire place : Ye burnte childe Dreadeth ye fyre; on beadsteads; Oh Sweete sleepe close myne eyes' or Avaunte ye nyghte mayre' English , old even to Chauceresque is adopted most properly to this most modern school.'[76]

4.33 Detail of mahogany bureau with copper panel and inscription. R1529

"WORDS ARE LIKE LEAVES AND WH-ERE THEY MOST ABOVND MVCH FRVIT of SENSE BENEATH IS RARELY FOVND"

4.34 Mahogany settle with copper panel and inscription. R1129

Figure 2 Some examples of mottoes used by Shapland and Petter

Inscription	Source	Item. R design number
Come Gentle Dreams the Hours of Sleep Beguile	Henry Wadsworth Longfellow, Poem *The Child Asleep*	Bed copper R7000
Sleep Doubtless and Secure	Shakespeare, *King John* 4. I	Bed copper R7052
Pleasant Dreams and Slumbers Light	To all to each a fair goodnight and pleasing dreams and slumbers light. Walter Scott, *L'Envory*	Bed carved R7161
In my Lady's Garden	Nursery Rhyme and Counting game. Harold Bell Wright	Bed bookcase stencilled R7051/2425
Weariness can Snore Upon the Flint When Resty Sloth Finds the Down Pillow Hard	Shakespeare, *Cymbeline* 3.6	White bed copper R7061
O Sleep it is a Gentle Thing	Samuel Coleridge Taylor, *The Rhyme of the Ancient Mariner.*	Bed carved and copper R7158
Sleep Gentle Sleep Nature's Soft Nurse	O Sleep O Gentle Sleep Natures Soft Nurse How have I frighted thee That thou no more wilt weigh my eyelids down. And steep my senses in forgetfulness. Shakespeare, *Henry 4 part 2 3. I*	Bed copper R7007
Night With Her Train of Stars and Her Great Gift of Sleep	Painting Robert Hughes 1912 W. E. Henley *Marguerita Sororis*	Bed copper R7160/7080
Vita Sine Literis Mors Est	A life without learning is death J Johnson Pettigrew 1847 Washington observatory	Copper book case large and small
The Sweet Serenity of Books	The love of learning, Sequestered nooks and all the sweet serenity of Books. Longfellow, *Morituri Salutamus*	Bookcase copper R1464/2420
Devise Wit Write Pen	Shakespeare, *Loves Labours Lost*	Desk, two separate copper panels R1550
Port After Storm	Port After Stormy Seas. Spencer, *The Faerie Queen*	Smokers cabinet copper R855
East West Homes Best	A commonplace expression	Settle, Hall Stand copper R1129/1140
Welcome Ever Smiles	Shakespeare, *Troilus and Cressida* 3. 3	Settle copper R1129
SALVE VALE	Good Health Farewell	Carved stencilled hall rober overmantel R1085/6017
Reading Maketh A Full Man	Bacon, *Of Studies* 1597	Bookcase copper R1463
Sublime Tobacco! Which from East to West Cheers the Tars Labours or the Turkman's Rest	Lord Byron, 1788-1824, *The Island* Canto ii Stanza 19	Bureau copper R848
Words Are Like Leaves and Where They Most Abound Much Fruit of Sense Beneath is Rarely Found	Pope, *Essays on Criticism* Pt 2	Bureau copper R1529
He Giveth His Beloved in Their Sleeping	He giveth unto His beloved in their sleep. Psalm 127:2	Bed copper conforming to R7000

4.35 Oak smoker's cabinet with copper panels and inscription. R848

4.36 Detail 4.35

4.37 Oak bookcase with copper
panel and inscription. R1463

Lettering as Ornament

A particularly important feature of inscriptions used by Shapland and Petter was the deliberately hand crafted style of lettering or calligraphy in which words were written. The lettering partially derived from styles of an earlier period in history and created with deliberate characteristics to fit the letters into an overall shape or frame which was aesthetically pleasing as well as simply spelling out the words. In some designs the flow of the inscription is punctuated by full stops placed in mid height between individual words, and a common practice was to fit in vowels changed in size in order to break up the regularity of the text and create a shape in keeping with the furniture design.

Another device used in lettering was the attenuation of vertical letters, which were stretched to span two lines at the start of the inscription. Long tall letters were a characteristic of the Glasgow School calligraphy exhibited by Frances and Margaret Macdonald in the late 1890's.[77] Another technique used by them and also Shapland and Petter was to draw out the horizontal lines or tails of letters E or L to underline words or other letters creating an integration of lettering into a balanced design.

Many examples of lettering in Arts and Crafts style existed on furniture and decorative objects from the period and it would not be difficult for any manufacturer to copy or adapt lettering designs. A book, *Lettering as Ornament* by F.R. Strange was included in a list of publications found in the Shapland and Petter archive. Another book on lettering is shown in an archive picture on a bookcase in their studio suggesting either or both may have been used as a source book.[78]

One further characteristic which was adopted in their lettering design was to substitute V for U as in their *HIGH CLASS FVRNITVRE* catalogue title. This was always used in latin and was a fairly common practice in depicting old script, Voysey had used it in his design for *The Studio* cover with the motto *VSE and BEAVTY*. The Bayeux Tapestry is a good example of the use of this convention and very similar lettering and presentation, which includes semi colons between words and part of the design.[79]

Hearts are for love

The most commonly used design in all Shapland and Petter's work was the heart, most frequently as an aperture pierced through wooden sides or supports in furniture or as a motif in beaten copper, as inlay, or enamelled panel. Hinges, handles and escutcheons were also heart shaped in several different designs. In Arts and Crafts decoration generally, the heart is the single most popular motif and is universally recognised as the symbol of the movement.

Symbolic of love, honesty and devotion the heart was adopted by the most influential Arts and Crafts designers. Baillie Scott's designs for Ivedene built in 1893/4 in Douglas Isle of Man included a beaten copper chimney hood with two large hearts, and other similar designs which were published and introduced this motif to the public eye.[80] At about the same time Voysey created designs with heart motifs, his metalwork designs published in the *British Architect* in January 1895[81] featured heart shaped leaves and also the same design with bursting seedpod. See 4.23. In 1896 Voysey exhibited an oak chair with pierced heart in the Arts and Crafts Exhibition. This was followed by many designs for furniture, architectural features in doors and balustrades and in copper work for furniture.

The source of the heart motif could be traced much further back into English romantic literature and painting particularly the pre-Raphaelite Brotherhood but its adoption by the Arts and Crafts movement brought it a new lease of life for aesthetic purposes and also as a symbol of integrity and devotion. The emphasis within the movement from its earliest days was on truth, integrity, joy in labour and love.

Heart shaped designs had some typical forms. Baillie Scott used fat hearts generously bulbous at each side, Glasgow designer George Walton favoured the flattened or 'squashed' heart, and E.A. Taylor, also of the Glasgow school, employed the 'split' heart in his design. Liberty used the heart in their furniture designs, several items featuring a pierced squashed heart. Of all designs, the Voysey heart most readily provides an example of the shape and proportion used by Shapland and Petter. Though there are many variations of the heart design with different sizes, the shape in wood tends to be longer than it is broad with a definite point at the bottom, as opposed to a rounded curve. Designs impressed in copper fittings tend to more rounded and squashed in form. There are occasional exceptions, the stick stand with three pointed heart and chequer banded inlay being a particular example. See 4.41 One particularly

4.38 Photo archive. White enamelled bed with copper panel and inscription

striking use of the heart shape is in escutcheons and Shapland and Petter used small copper heart-shaped lock plates on much of their furniture, using a shape almost identical to that employed by Voysey in the escutcheons and other metal work designed for Thomas Elsley and Co.[82]

The inverted heart was also a commonly used design. The pierced splats used in beds, chairs and hall furniture have inverted hearts and are an easily recognisable feature of Shapland and Petter design. See Chapter 5 for further discussion.

Symbolism?

From the examples of the motifs used by Shapland and Petter it might be possible to assume they were used because of their religious significance. Symbols of the peacock and the lotus feature strongly in Shapland and Petter designs and it could be more than coincidental that these symbols linked to important Christian beliefs of life after death and the resurrection of Christ. Shapland and Petter and a number of their employees including key men such as Cowie and Seyfert were devout Plymouth Brethren and it would be easy to attribute to them motivation to include symbolic images in decorative design.

Important sources of influence were nearby as Barnstaple man and Arts and Crafts pioneer W.R. Lethaby wrote his very scholarly study of mysticism and symbolism in architecture published in 1892, which was said to have been drawn upon keenly by Charles Rennie Mackintosh.[83] At the turn of the century, the popularity of movements which embraced secret symbolism such as the Theosophists and the Rosicrucians makes it tempting to speculate whether the use of the rose, heart, lotus and the lily, and the often heraldic like placement of these symbols on furniture represented some secret or coded message. More research is needed on this subject.

4.39 Heart shaped escutcheon and impressed handle by Loach and Clarke

4.41 Oak stick stand with 'chequer inlay' and pierced hearts. R1088

4.40 Oak bedroom chair. Suite T428

4.42 Oak firescreen with pierced hearts and copper panel. R1894

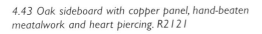

4.43 Oak sideboard with copper panel, hand-beaten meatalwork and heart piercing. R2121

Chapter 5 Construction Materials and Techniques

5.1 Hall seat with glove box. Side on view. R1073.

It should be fairly clear from the last chapter that Shapland and Petter developed a distinctive house style in terms of the vocabulary of motifs and ornament which they used in the Arts and Crafts range. In addition to this applied 'artistic' decoration there are other important distinguishing features relating to construction which are definitive of the Shapland and Petter style. This chapter looks at some typical structural characteristics such as the squared spindles and the geometric arches which appear to be almost unique to Shapland and Petter, or at least strongly associated with their work but with no other known manufacturer. Attention is also given to the practical and craft elements of the creation of their furniture, which include inlaid design, copper work and enamelling, all of which were done at the Raleigh Cabinet Works in Barnstaple.

Materials; the woods

'The Coal Boxes illustrated in this Catalogue are made of Fumed Wainscot Oak, Walnut or Mahogany. Some are supplied in richly figured Brown Oak, and less expensive patterns in Kauri Pine or Ash stained, seasoned wood being selected in all cases.'

Shapland and Petter Raleigh catalogue[84]

Most of the furniture made at the Raleigh works in Barnstaple was made either in oak, mahogany, ash or walnut with occasional mention of the use of hazelwood, satinwood and greywood in the catalogues. There is some evidence that pine was used for bedroom furniture but this tended not to be in the Arts and Crafts range. Ash stained green was used occasionally, and oak (and mahogany) was fumed for some pieces, i.e. darkened by exposure to ammonia fumes in a sealed chamber. White painted furniture was also an option used particularly for highly decorated bedroom furniture and occasionally for desks, in the catalogues this was described as 'Enamelled Ivory White' Other wood mentioned includes rosewood or 'silver grey' for bookcases, greywood for cabinets, amboyna for coal boxes and birch and burl for bedroom suites. Prices ran from brown oak, the most expensive, to mahogany, then wainscot oak, walnut and ash or other. Cabinets made in mahogany with satinwood margins were also top of the range.

It is interesting to note references in catalogues to 'brown oak' which is most probably English brown oak (*Quercus petraea*), one of the rarest woods in the world.[85]

Oak used for most Arts and Crafts pieces was described as wainscot oak which was probably sourced from both America

perpendicular lines, squared moulding of rhomboid diamond shapes standing on their points and clean compass drawn curves give the essential character.

There is also a powerful three dimensional presence for more decorative pieces, which avoids, for example, the temptation to present a wardrobe as a box with decoration. Projecting cupboards, horizontal curved shelves or drawers break the flat plane, overhanging cornices with supporting brackets which continue to the sides take the eye round the structure. A test of the quality of design is to view pieces from the side rather than the front and very often this shows the powerful structural features as well as an elegance in the line and sense of proportion. The monotony of blank spaces and straight lines is carefully avoided with the addition of brackets, slatted rows, pierced shapes, curved and angled apertures.

Frames and panels

The frame and panel system of construction of many pieces not only provided the framework into which the functions of storage in drawers, shelves, hooks and rails are accommodated but also the frame into which decorative panels were set. The Shapland and Petter style of construction in this respect appears to have followed an innovation which emanates from C.R. Ashbee. In

5.2 Oak bedside cabinet with inlaid Glasgow roses. From the Suite R214

and Europe. The term wainscot oak was used synonymously with Baltic oak which referred to oak from Poland and the wide area around the Baltic Sea. With wainscot oak, the way the oak was sawn was the essential characteristic, rather than its origin. Wainscot oak was 'quarter sawn' i.e. logs are sliced into four quarters and then planks cut from each quarter right on the 90 degree mark to reveal lighter yellow or orange streaks known as medullary rays across the long running grain. Whilst the precise identification of woods is beyond the scope of this book, much of the oak used appears to be American red oak (*Quercus rubra*) and with Austrian wainscot oak as identified in a contemporary reference work.[86] Some pieces observed appear to have American red oak for frames and sides with panels in more highly figured Austrian oak, carefully selected for grain and colour as was always the case with Shapland and Petter. There is also some probability that brown oak was used in conjunction with Austrian and or American red oak.

Structural

Though a fair proportion of Shapland and Petter pieces in Arts and Crafts style reflected the curved shapes of earlier styles the more definitive pieces followed a strong geometric line in their design. Rectangular frames and panels, angled arches, strong

5.3 Mahogany bed with inlaid tulip design. R7002

discussing the construction techniques of the Guild of Handicraft, Alan Crawford draws attention to the influence of Ashbee in changing the convention by fixing panels into their frames from the back, with pinned moulding, rather than from the front.[87] Shapland and Petter used this technique frequently, for wood panels and for copper though with the latter a moulded front edge to the frame was often used. The consequence of putting the panel into a square edged frame from the back is that the panel meets the frame at a clean right angle rather than a curve, strengthening the geometric effect. In this construction the area of doors is broken up into two planes of panels and frames one recessed behind the other, giving greater visual interest.

Squared spindles and moulded columns

Within their house style, horizontal rails or galleries along the back or sides of pieces are supported by rows of spindles. This was a very common technique of the period and earlier periods, but Shapland and Petter created their own style here, using squared spindles. Perhaps their best known features are the rows of squared tapering spindles which vary in length from 35cms to 8cms and are shaped with gentle curves on each of four sides. Shapland and Petter referred to these as *'square wrought spindles.'*[88] These required special machine technology to create, and the 'Thurming'[89] machines which cut these sections and the longer square moulded sections for vertical supports are referred to in a contemporary description of the workshops in Chapter 2. No other Arts and Crafts furniture maker appears to have used this technique to create square moulded spindles or used spindles squared or otherwise to such a great effect as that achieved by Shapland and Petter.

The manufacture of the square moulded column was also a technical achievement in that it required special machinery to mould (or carve) a shaped design on each of the four faces on the square section. Many manufacturers used tapered columns as vertical supports which floated off but supported the main structure, particularly in fire surrounds, settles and bookcases. The columns used by Shapland and Petter were distinctive with square profiles featuring straight and/or curved tapering decorative caps and feet either as blocks or pads. Some of the moulded designs on the columns resembled thistle or bud like shapes, and caps or tops of verticals were also sometimes given a bud shape. Again these shaped caps were used by other manufacturers but made separately then stuck on with dowels to the main column, rather than made as one piece as Shapland and Petter were able to do.

The strong emphasis on vertical supports provides structural strength but also gave the opportunity to show off square moulding techniques at which Shapland and Petter excelled.

Tapering columns, capped verticals and pad feet were features which strongly defined Arts and Crafts style.

Another particular structural technique employed was the use of pierced splats to support rails and galleries on chairs, hall tables and hall stands and also on finer pieces such as music or display cabinets. The most easily recognised shape is that of the splat shaped as a thick stemmed bud pierced with an inverted heart, and these splats arranged in rows of three or more. This shape was not unique to Shapland and Petter, designs by C.H.B. Quennell for J.P. White and for Heals show near identical forms, and the advertisements published by Heals for their St Ives bedroom furniture show a bed with heart pierced splats.[90] The first appearance of this design in work by Shapland and Petter was for a coal box shown in a feature about the company in 1899.[91]

A virtually exclusive feature in their construction was the geometric arch, pointed at the top rather than curved and frequently constructed with four angled and perfectly mitred sections. Similar examples of this arch have been observed in published designs of other companies, but only rarely and no company appears to have used this as a regular feature. Many examples exist of this arch by Shapland and Petter and it provides a strong geometric character to the structures, distinguishing their pieces from rival companies which persisted with the curved arch which was easier and cheaper to produce. Another characteristic arch was the curved arch with two 'teeth' either side used for aprons for chairs and hall stands, and for the open cupboard spaces for wardrobes. See 2.11. No examples have been identified of this shape being used by other manufacturers.

Wavy Moulding

The technique which above all was responsible for the early success of the Shapland and Petter business, was the creation of wavy or ripple moulding. In Chapter 2 the importance of this innovation to the business in the 1850s was explained and it is very interesting to observe that it still played an important role in design and construction 50 years later. The pieces illustrated 4.33 and 6.26 dating from around the turn of the century were much enhanced by the moulding used, in both cases the wood appears to be rosewood which looks equally well with oak or mahogany. The use of moulding to secure panels in frames from the front was not generally used by Shapland and Petter who, as we've seen, tended to machine a moulded edge to the frame itself and insert the panel from the back into a rebated edge with nailed beading. The use of wavy moulding is the only known exception to the usual practice of securing panels from the reverse rather than the front.

5.4 Oak settle with squared spindles and moulded columns. R1146

Quality of construction

Throughout the whole range of their work the quality of cabinet making and construction was meticulous. Joints fit perfectly and are held with pegs or tenons for lasting strength, rather than fixed with nails or glue blocks. Metalwork is always fitted with care, with the right size screws, locks and hinges are well made and always sunk into the wood with precision. Some techniques which are associated with Shapland and Petter are the construction of drawers using ash as a secondary wood for sides and linings giving strength, and also the hidden dovetails at the back of drawers, rather than glued at the side giving strong and smooth running drawers. Fixing of drawer backs in this way gave them longevity, locking the sides in place and providing resistance to sides coming apart if exposed to damp conditions. Fixing of wooden panels was also done with consideration, panels being held in place by moulding rather being screwed or nailed, and thus allowing the panel to shrink with age yet not split along the grain. Fitted backs for wardrobe and other large pieces are invariably of panelled construction often in ash, or plain oak.

5.6 Chair with square moulded legs. R1150.

5.5 Smokers Table with thistle shaped section of column and beaten copper top. R904

5.7 oak hall table with copper panel and square moulded legs. R1407

Metalwork

Much of the character of Shapland and Petter Arts and Crafts pieces derives from the copper panels, hinges, lock plates and handles which provide the medieval and artistic character. The copper panels are perhaps the most recognisable feature of their style, but hinges with beaten or impressed hearts and repoussé design add power and charisma. Finer pieces have silvered metalwork on hinges and, on some pieces, decorative panels are inlaid with pewter.

Throughout their range, the metalwork used on Shapland and Petter furniture was invariably of a high standard. Solid brass two lever locks inset into the wood were the standard rather than steel locks screwed in place from the back. Solid copper panels and handles were always used and never the cheaper alternatives of anodised or coppered steel to appear as if copper. The choice of good quality fittings in solid brass or copper for hooks, hinges, and hanging rails, and solid copper screws for fixing decorative features increased cost but maintained the quality and durability of the furniture.

Hinges, handles and lock plates

Medieaval character was assigned to heavier oak pieces through the use of long strap hinges, often with sinuous lines and impressed heart design and many versions have been observed, some of which may have been inspired by Voysey and Baillie Scott designs. Handles and lock plate escutcheons tended to complement the design of hinges, and the full visual effect of the metalwork is invariably carefully matched and weighted to the piece. In most cases copper work was presented with an antique 'oxidised' finish but there are several examples of silvered copper, such as the hinges illustrated 5.14, and occasionally gilded work on fine cabinets 5.13.

A fairly wide variety of handles was used by Shapland and Petter but some patterns were more frequently used than others. The illustration 5.10 shows some popular models which are thought to have been commissioned by them for their exclusive use. The most common is that with the 'L&C' stamp (see 4.39) which is the trademark for Loach and Clarke, metal workers based in

5.8 Oak settle with copper panel and pierced splats. R1145

Birmingham (often mistakenly assumed to mean Liberty, see Chapter 6). Shapland and Petter accounts in the ledger for the turn of the century show purchases from this supplier and one could surmise that much of the bulk and bespoke metalwork was commissioned from this firm to be used exclusively on their furniture.

Other handles regularly used were occasionally marked on the back plate with stamped registered design numbers which have been traced to metalworkers and brass founders who registered their designs. Hinges too have makers' marks occasionally but no connections with significant designers have been identified through these marks to date, and the assumption is that most metalwork was bought from trade suppliers as a routine procurement.

A commonly used set of metalwork was that which was used the bureau illustrated 2.1, consisting of long strap hinges, matching handles and lock plates with crimped or piecrust edges. These

5.9 Detail of metalwork from oak buffet. R2134

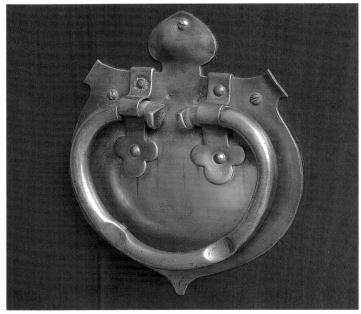

5.10 Examples of copper and brass handles used by Shapland and Petter with cast and machine pressed construction

have a hand beaten appearance but are clearly made in batches to conform to a pattern (this does not rule out the possibility that they were made by hand) and have been observed with the stamp 'C&A' on the reverse which is the mark for Crofts and Assinder of Birmingham.[92]

Whilst the majority of metalwork appeared to be batch-made by machine pressing or casting, there are examples of metalwork which are clearly hand made, bearing hammer marks and irregularities which provide a tactile and visual impression of more ancient and possibly medieaval origin. These 'Hand Beaten metal mounts' as referred to in Shapland and Petter's catalogue

for *Coal Boxes*[93] are clear evidence that the company straddled the divide between mechanised production and handicraft, being able to blend both into the finished product with great effect.

Unfortunately no evidence has come to light to indicate where this metalwork was carried out, though there is a strong probability that it was done in a workshop on site, (see below re repoussé copper panels).

Hand-beaten or hand-wrought fittings include hinges and handles and tended to be used on more richly decorated pieces. Some of these fittings are unusual in that they are made of brass

5.11 Examples of hand-beaten metalwork believed to be original to Shapland and Petter furniture

which when naturally patinated through age looks very similar to copper. Another distinguishing feature is that the edges are hand planished to produce small and regular indentations as a decorative finish. Droppers and rings of handles are also hand-beaten to produce an attractive angular surface. No identification marks have been observed on these fittings.

Grilles

A frequently employed technique in the finer pieces which included glass panes was to cover these with copper 'grilles' or tracery which consisted of a fine pattern cut from a sheet of copper and placed over the glass. The copper grille was often silvered and examples found today tend to have lost most of the silvering as a result of polishing. A published review described these as 'oxidised silver grilles'[94] These grilles appear to be hand made and have been given a convex, partially rounded front, similar to leaded work in stained glass. Whilst some designs for these grilles have 'art nouveau' stylised plant forms, there are examples of the designs which feature hearts, interwoven foliage and buds are similar to designs observed in repoussé copper panels.

5.13 *Gilded escutcheon on mahogany display cabinet*

5.12 *Oak smokers cabinet with repoussé design of honesty seed pods. R921*

Locks

In most cases drawers and doors were fitted with brass locks, and invariably these were stamped S&PB often with the words Secure Lever added. Locks used tended to be two lever and were neatly fitted, flush into the wood of the door or drawer. Smaller items such a smokers cabinets have been observed to have locks without S&PB stamps (See Chapter 7).

Repoussé Copper panels

The techniques of copper repoussé work were fairly widely disseminated during the last few years of the nineteenth century. Articles on the Newlyn School of Industrial Art which specialised in repoussé copper work and on the techniques of repoussé work were published in *The Studio, British Architect* and *Art Workers Quarterly*.[95] Copper work was particularly popular in local craft workshops of the type established through the Home Arts Industries and there appeared to be a ready market for well executed pieces, throughout Liberty, Guild of Handicraft and other shops in London nearby to Berners Street.

In Barnstaple, metalworking crafts were taught at the Barnstaple School of Art and the skills of 'art' metalworking were clearly available to Shapland and Petter locally before the end of the nineteenth century. The establishment of the Barnstaple Guild of Metalworkers, linked to the School of Art added to the pool of craftsmanship available (see Chapter 6)

The application of copper panels to decorate furniture has precedent in the Arts and Crafts movement in designs by Baillie Scott. Furniture sold at Liberty designed by Leonard Wyburd featured inset copper panels thought to be executed by ex Guild

5.14 *Silvered metalwork on doors from inlaid mahogany cabinet*

5.15 Coalbox with copper mounts. Furniture Record August 1904

5.16 'Quaint' coal vase in mahogany and burnished copper. R1962

of Handicraft artist and craftsman John Pearson. However, no company appears to have made such extensive use of this form of ornament as Shapland and Petter. A number of cabinet makers did use repoussé panels and their work was shown in trade periodicals. Harris Lebus for example used machine pressed copper panels, one popular version for a bedroom suite depicting Viking ships and bearing a stamped registered design number.

Evidence suggests that copper panels used by Shapland and Petter were hand made, within the works at Barnstaple. Inspection of panel backs shows hand chasing to create the outline of the pattern, with occasional pencil marks and small pierced holes where the panel has been fixed during the process of being worked. There do not appear to be many examples of panels with chased decoration to add detail to the front, only one example has been observed, that of stork or heron in a hallstand. Virtually all panels have impressed designs from the back, presumably hand hammered onto pitch. Panels made in pairs or in threes are clearly not identical and there are occasional examples of variations or departures from the design which are not concealed but reconciled within the design, very much in the same way as hand knotted Persian rugs. Panels and copper work were 'oxidised' to give an antique patina rather than sold with shiny new looking copper. The ledger for Shapland and Petter shows costs for acids to create this oxidised finish.

A most interesting review of Shapland and Petter in 1903 referred to their decorative crafts:-

'We may say we were surprised to learn that all the repoussé work and much of the enamelling is executed at the firms own works.'[96]

Another reviewer was similarly impressed with a firescreen:-

'The screen may be had in wainscot oak or mahogany and has a hand beaten oxidised copper panel. These hand beaten panels enter into the composition of many of the screens the firm are showing and are combined with a centre panel of bronzed leaded glass in very effective designs.'[97]

The references to copper and enamel work here are particularly intriguing. In the introduction to the catalogue for coal boxes we are told that :-

'The copper panels (where this form of decoration is employed) are beaten entirely by hand, thereby imparting an artistic surface to the metal, impossible by any other means.'[98]

This review also makes reference to 'delicately modelled hand beaten copper panels'

5.17 Mahogany smokers cabinet with copper grille. R845

Enamelling

The technique of enamelling, or applying coloured glass to metal as decoration has been recognised as one of the highest level of skills within the decorative arts with a tradition which goes back a long way before the Arts and Crafts movement. Enamelling is one of the oldest decorative arts and one of the most permanent. Early enamellers in Britain included Celtic and Roman craftsmen and by medieaval times the craft was well advanced.

A high level of artistic skill is required to represent pictorial and ornamental designs in colour and this is achieved through complex technical skill to apply the enamel itself by firing in a kiln or by blowtorch. Arts and Crafts designers who have created superb examples of enamelling include Alexander Fisher, F.C Varley Nelson Dawson and many others. Ashbee in particular was pictured in *The Studio* in front of his enamelling kiln at the Guild of Handicraft in 1897[99] and there were fine examples of the craft exhibited at the Arts and Crafts Exhibition in London. Metalwork with enamelling was on sale at Liberty in the Tudric and Cymric ranges from about 1898. A copper fireplace hood designed by Baillie Scott for Darmstadt was pictured in *The Studio* described as *'Rich with repoussé copper and enamels.'*[100]

Barnstaple School of Art was clearly engaged in teaching and producing enamelling as examples of metalwork and jewellery with inset enamels were featured in *British Architect* and *The Studio* from the beginning of the twentieth century. (See Chapter 6) At some point probably between 1900 and 1902, the designers at Shapland and Petter decided to introduce enamelling into their range of techniques for furniture decoration and by April 1903 their exciting new range was reviewed in the *Furniture Record* with glowing appreciation:-

'The metal fittings are of antique copper, relieved by vitreous enamel, giving jewel-like effects in the light. The firm have evidently given much consideration to this matter of embellishment and have evolved some original effects. The new decorative panels in colour and this enamelling on copper are among them. The latter is carried out with charming results in picture panels, in which the copper is worked up by the hammer into a relief design, representing say a landscape and the colour effects introduced by translucent enamelling. These panels are employed to embellish sideboards, wardrobes and cabinets with excellent taste, and in wall mirrors finished in white enamel.'[101]

5.18 Walnut log box with copper panels and hand-wrougt handles. R1976

5.19 Oak hall table with copper panel. R1072

1072 3ft. Carved, Inlaid or Copper panel.

5.20 Oak desk with copper panels. R1550

5.21 Oak bed with copper panel and inscription

This tantalising account confirms that some very special pieces were made with enamelling but to date, few have been recorded. The most common enamels found on contemporary pieces are inset enamelled hearts and panels with mixed colours of red blue and green which are used in bookcases and bedroom furniture. Rarer pieces exist such as the sideboard with hand made lock plate and inset enamelled panel in red. See 5.26. A very special piece, illustrated is the bookcase with large copper panel inset with green enamel panels and plant forms enamelled in single colours of red, blue and green. See 5.25. This is Shapland and Petter at their very best. To date no larger pictorial panels of the sort described have been identified. By 1905 enamelling appears to have been an established technique for the embellishment of furniture handles. A review describes a sideboard with '*Metal fittings enriched with translucent enamels.*'[102]

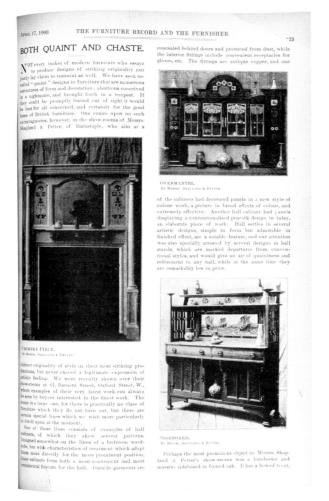

5.22 Furniture Record April 1903

5.23 Furniture Record June 1905

5.24 White dressing chest with inlaid Glasgow roses and inset enamel discs. R429

Ceramic tiles and panels

The incorporation of tiles into furniture has a long tradition of use for functional and aesthetic reasons. The functional use of tiles was mainly to protect against ingress of water in washstands or hall furniture and the purely aesthetic use for decoration covers a wide range of applications where pictorial and patterned or simply coloured tiles were used. Shapland and Petter used tiles referred to as 'ceramic panels' for many of their pieces and also applied ceramic discs or panels for Arts and Crafts pieces. The tiles used ranged from the routine to the exquisite and a range of suppliers appear to have been used including Pilkington's, the Decorative Art Tile Company and Della Robbia, each is mentioned in the ledgers.

Interesting examples of the most decorative tiles discovered to date are a Dutch scene, the Medmenham fruiting tree,[103] the lady on horseback, and 'Chance' by Eleanor Fortescue Brickdale.

5.25 Oak bookcase with copper panel with inscription VITA SINE LITERIS MORS EST and centre panel with applied enamelling. R2420

5.26 Oak sideboard with hand-beaten brass panels and handles with enamelled lock plate. See also 5.11.

5.28 Oak wall cabinet with Medmenham Pottery ceramic panels. R858a

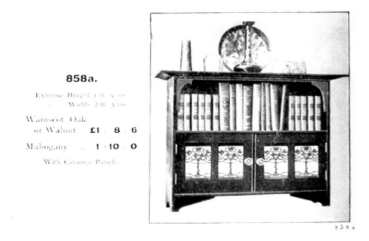

858a.

Extreme Height 1 ft. 9 ins.
    Width 2 ft. 3 ins.

Wainscot Oak
or Walnut   £1 : 8 : 6

Mahogany ... 1 : 10 : 0

With Ceramic Panels

858a

5.29 High Class Furniture Wall Cabinets

See 4.1, 4.15, 5.28 and 5.30. The last three tiles are particularly interesting as they are unusual and would not have been produced as a large commercial run but rather as hand crafted and limited edition. The fruiting tree pattern which resembles an apple or lemon tree has been observed as part of a larger tiled panel from the Medmenham Pottery, created by Conrad Dressler, sculptor and founder of the Della Robbia Pottery.[104] Whilst there is a reference in the ledger to Della Robbia as a supplier to Shapland and Petter there is no further evidence to confirm exactly what they supplied (Della Robbia was also a supplier of marble as well as ceramics). The tile showing the lady on horseback, see 4.1, shows a very similar style of construction and decoration i.e. 'dust pressed' and could also be from the Medmenham pottery though there is no evidence for this.

The tile designed by Eleanor Fortescue Brickdale is used in an absolutely perfect setting. As the central focus of the smokers cabinet it creates a romantic and passionate image, with Pre-Raphaelite theme and some Glasgow style suggested with the rose in the headband. The archive photograph of this piece is in black and white and gives no hint of the beautiful colour and effect achieved in the glaze.

Tiles were used in table tops, trays, hallstands and washstands and in some cases the selection of these was particularly sensitive to the image and the effect created, the leaf and berry design in the tray shown, and the rose shown against a pink background for the tiles in the white bedroom suite are good examples (Illustration 4.27). The rose tiles on this suite have the mark for Pilkingtons on the reverse.

The use of ceramic panels was not a common form of decoration of Arts and Crafts furniture. Liberty featured metalwork with inset heart shaped and circular panels, described as 'porcelain ornament'[105] There are some examples of furniture made in the Glasgow School tradition which were decorated with ceramic inserts but only Shapland and Petter seemed to make frequent use of ceramics in this way. The most commonly observed form is the blue, green, or orange and red ceramic discs inset into bedroom furniture. The photo archive also shows different shaped inserts in a bed and large discs in a hallstand. The glazes observed have mottled effect which is similar to Ruskin pottery, and whilst these are often referred to as 'Ruskins', there is evidence that this is not the case. Made of white pipeclay they appear similar to ceramics made by Brannam in Barnstaple, mentioned as a supplier in the Shapland and Petter ledgers. However, a single green panel, examined by the author did have a registered design number in relief on the back and research at the Public Records Office provided confirmation that the design was registered by Pilkingtons.[106]

5.30 Mahogany smokers cabinet with copper hinges and ceramic panel by Eleanor Fortescue Brickdale. R862

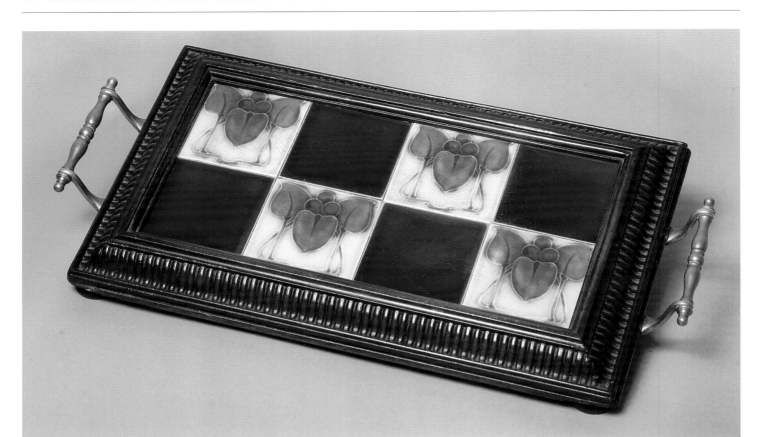

5.35 Tray with tiles and original label to reverse

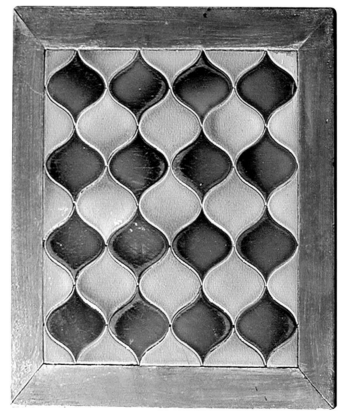

5.36 Tiled table top; mahogany table. R1763

5.37 Mahogany stick stand with copper panel and tiled back. R1035

5.38 Oak dressing chest with inset ceramic panels. R162 of Suite R152

5.39 Oak wardrobe with ceramic panels and copper panels in Glasgow rose design. R152

Carved Decoration

Shapland and Petter employed teams of highly skilled carvers in the period before Arts and Crafts became popular and their work is referred to in Chapter 2. As fashion changed towards the end of the nineteenth century, inlaid and copper panels became desirable instead of carving and a preference for 'plain oak furniture' with a rustic rather than ornate look was established. Despite changing trends some Arts and Crafts pieces were decorated by carving and the catalogue indicates a range of items were available 'with hand worked copper' or 'carved panel'. Items described as 'handsomely carved' or 'richly carved' were still being advertised in the catalogue of circa 1905 or later but these designs were traditional and not in the new art style.

Examples of carving as decoration for Arts and Crafts pieces do exist; the chair 5.41 and hall robe panels illustrated 5.40 show the style and quality of the work. Very attractive examples with

Glasgow rose design and other plant forms have been observed on settles, hall cupboards and sideboards. The carved decoration which has been observed has been achieved by carving away the background and leaving the pattern standing out from the background in relief. Considerable skill would have been required to create the hall robe panels shown.

Stencilled and Painted Panels

Shapland and Petter created stencilled picture panels using semi-transparent colours, which look similar to coloured inks in those examples which have been observed. Several stencilled pieces were illustrated in their catalogues and in the archives, and some are very similar to those used by Liberty. Stencilling was featured as a decorative art in contemporary art journals, *The Studio*, for

5.40 Carved panels in oak hall robe in restoration.

5.41 Oak hall chair with carved design. R1408

example, in 1903 included an article with pictures of stencilled panels by Hugh Wallis, one showing a scene very similar to a Chaucerian inspired panel by Shapland and Petter.[107]

In the Shapland and Petter catalogues these panels were described as 'Coloured Stencilled Panel' and 'Decorated Wood Panel'. Some panels appeared to be fairly large, up to a metre in length and perhaps the most elaborate panel was that shown on a sideboard in the review of the company in 1903.

'One of the cabinets had decorated panels in a new style of colour work, a picture in broad effects of colour and extremely effective.'[108]

The panel about one metre long depicts three sailing ships on a swelling sea, (Illustration 5.22) while another large panel of pilgrims on horseback was used in an oak settle shown in the photo archive. The precise method of creating these picture panels is uncertain, clearly the picture started with a stencilled outline which was then hand coloured, with emphasis given to particular lines to increase definition. Coloured wood stains appear to have been the medium used, covered with a coat of clear shellac. The panels appear to be of sycamore or in some cases, of oak. Colours do not appear to have been able to stand exposure to prolonged sunlight or to water without some measure of deterioration.

Gesso or moulded panels

A rare form of decoration which appears to have been used in later years of the Arts and Crafts period is the painted gesso panel. In a slightly sarcastic review of 'new art' furniture in 1903, the reviewer complained:-

5.42 Detail stencilled panel, oak bureau bookcase. 4.13; R1541

'Panels are used to a considerable extent. Here however, woodcarving is somewhat out of vogue, for it is considered rather old fashioned, a sort of wallowing in antiquity, and consequently recourse is to hammered copper or Gesso. As regards the latter medium, Gesso, its artistic effect is vastly intensified by the romance of its name and nature (which like the new light, the higher cult itself) is sealed from the ken of common mortality. Is not romance made up of a sense of mystery? Well, Gesso is very artistic, and that is the point.'[109]

Only two examples of this panel work by Shapland and Petter have been identified to date, 'To Share Our Treasures', and the Village Band. Each were on simple and elegant bookcases with very attractive effect. On examination of these panels they appear to be made of papier mache or some form of

5.43 Mahogany bookcase with leaded lights, opalescent glass and decorative panel. R2431

5.44 Detail of 5.43

5.45 Oak bookcase with decorative panel. R2467

compressed paper, pressed into a shallow mould then painted, rather than a gesso. It is presumed that the word gesso, was used as a generic term to describe moulded work. The panels are in shallow relief and may have been produced by a patent process similar to Lincrusta or to that for embossing leather. Observation of two different panels depicting the same scene indicated they were identical i.e. from the same mould rather than individually crafted as in the copper panels. No references to or pictures of these panels in the Shapland and Petter archive have been discovered to date.

Leaded and Stained Glass

There is range of pieces which feature leaded 'lights' and stained glass, usually in fine cabinets and bookcases but occasionally in screens and firescreens. A small writing table was produced with

Glasgow Style glass panel described as 'Decorative Glazed Screen Back' and a desk with elaborate inlay and leaded glass panel also seemed to be produced in some numbers as several examples survive. Clear glass used in panels e.g. the mahogany smokers cabinet illustrated 5.17 was reeded and faintly tinted and described as Cathedral Glass. It is not known where these were made and nor where the materials came from. In the main panels were clear with an inner panel of coloured glass design. A particularly attractive feature was the use of ovals and hearts in opalescent glass in leaded lights. These features in pink or blue-green glass have a beautiful and delicate colouring and are used with restraint as if they were precious stones.

Lead in leaded glass was often given a patination and this was described in the catalogues as 'Bronzed Leaded Glass'. The firescreens with glass panels also had copper panels to the side and the catalogue made the point that ' Coloured Glass Introduced into this screen is exceptionally fine.'[110] The work on the firescreen illustrated 5.47 shows a high level of craftsmanship in the creation of the overall picture and the detail.

Other techniques

Other decorative panels in ceramics, silk, and tapestry were also used but no examples of these in Arts and Crafts style have been observed to date.

Inlay, Marquetry and Intarsia

Of all the decorative techniques used by Shapland and Petter the inlaid work is perhaps the finest and most elegant. Inlaid work required a depth of knowledge and considerable artistic and craft skills. There are many examples which range from the most simple inlaid chequer banding of light and dark woods to the elaborate pictorial designs rendered in rare and coloured woods with metal and mother of pearl inlay. No other British manufacturer seems to have produced such a wide range of inlaid furniture decorated in Arts and Crafts style to such a high standard in design, colour and execution.

5.46 Detail of 5.45

5.47 Mahogany firescreen with leaded glass panel. R1894

1894 FIRESCREEN
26 x 33

The techniques of inlay and marquetry go back to the Renaissance and before that. To be clear about the techniques, we can refer to Henry Percival Shapland, (grandson of Henry P Shapland) who in 1926 gave the following explanation in his masterful description of the subject:

'The terms inlay and marquetry are at present used rather loosely and perhaps need some definition. Strictly speaking inlaid work should be regarded as a technique which consists of forming slight sinkings of an eighth or a quarter of an inch deep in the solid wood, and then filling the hollows so made with woods of a different colour, cut to fit them. Marquetry is a later development and is closely bound up with veneering. In Marquetry the ornament is first cut into a thin sheet of wood or veneer and subsequently the veneer and ornament, as one sheet, is applied to the surface of the wood. There is a third term tarsia or intarsia. It should be used to designate those pictorial effects in wood in the production of which the craftsman used the utmost skill and chose his material with the greatest care, in order to vie as far as possible with the work of painters.'[111]

Shapland and Petter used each of these techniques to create the most excellent adornment of their best pieces and even routine items such as pot cupboards and coal boxes were richly decorated. Contemporary reviews of their work often included praise for the skill, artistry and innovative approach.

5.48 Mahogany bureau and music cabinet with inlaid design of honesty seed pods. R1537

5.49 Panel detail from Shapland and Petter wardrobe inlaid with copper and abalone

'Inlaid work in English made furniture is, no doubt capable of a great deal of development. Few, if any, firms pay more attention to this subject than Shapland and Petter, Ltd. as the contents of their Showrooms at Berners Street, W. prove. Much of the furniture to be seen here is enriched with inlay work and develops new ideas in this direction.'[112]

Inlay

Inlaid work was produced in all of the hardwoods used and designs were usually limited in size confined to small panels excavated into the surface and filled with a pattern of different material to create the design. Inlaid work frequently used shell described as 'Mother o'Pearl' and abalone, a mottled blue grey shell. Inlaid designs are often found in conjunction with chequer banding, inlaid with dark and light wood.

The careful selection and restrained placement of these shell pieces provided jewel-like effect in decoration, concentrating the eye with precision on the beauty of nature in the shimmering iridescent colours of blue, green and red abalone and translucent silvery white mother of pearl. These materials are used as part of designs mixed with wood and metal, often as segments in a geometric pattern and within their own settings in emblematic shapes of hearts, honesty seed pods, lotus flowers and stylised forms. The inlaid copper work shown in 5.49 is a fine example of this style of decoration.

5.50 Detail mahogany display cabinet. R2027

5.51 Mahogany bedside cupboard inlaid design. R109

Marquetry work

This decorative technique was used to great effect in the finer cabinets, revolving bookcases, and bedroom suites often in mahogany. Large scale designs in panels of up to 1 metre long and 50/60 centimetres wide were made, featuring stylised floral designs and the peacock pattern which was a particular favourite for cabinets and hall robes inlaid in woods and shell. The mirror illustrated with stylised peacock feathers is constructed with a single sheet of veneer 66 centimetres wide, pierced to receive the inlaid design. See 4.17.

A wide variety of woods were used for inlaid design including rosewood, partridge wood, yew tree and satinwood. There was virtually no limit to the shades achieved from natural woods from black through warm browns, reds and yellows to the white of holly or sycamore which were often stained, particularly in green and also other colours. Engraving was used to create detail in the more pictorial pieces such as the peacock designs.

A key characteristic of marquetry was the repetition of the design and scrolling decoration which covered fairly large panels, and then repeated on smaller items i.e. as in bedroom suites. The need to cut multiple pieces of inlay of identical shape was most probably managed by the use of a particular machine called a 'donkey' described in Chapter 2. Apart from the donkey the process was in the hands of the craftsman, and clearly a high level of craft skill was required, far remote from mechanisation. Skill

in matching colour, and in cutting to create an exact fit of the pattern into the ground are evident in the work. Whilst variations from the pattern are not uncommon in designs, appearing perhaps as mistakes, it is the lack of absolute mechanical precision which gives these pieces integrity and individuality as handicraft and art.[113]

Intarsia

The construction of picture panels with coloured woods was an Italian technique, and in a sense not inlay at all as the whole panel depicts a picture made up of a variety of woods chosen to 'paint' the scene. In medieaval Europe, Siena was regarded as the centre of the marquetry cutters. Much of the best work was made by monks, who excelled in the portrayal of building and landscapes in perspective. Shapland quotes a contemporary description of a craftsmen in intarsia:-

'He was such a genius as is to be found in the whole world in putting together wood with so much art that they appear to be pictures made with a brush.'[114]

It is not surprising that Shapland and Petter wished to develop their expertise in this area given their years of dealing in veneers and the skill and experience of their craftsmen in creating veneered work. It is interesting however to consider why some Arts and Crafts pieces were decorated with pictures of continental scenes, and it may be that this was the influence of Christopher William Deubler, German master craftsman who was the inlay and marquetry specialist working for Shapland and Petter. In the pictorial scenes created by Deubler we can see the very finest work of the company, the richness and warmth of colour combined with superbly elegant design putting these pieces at the top of the hierarchy of Arts and Crafts work at the turn of the nineteenth century.

5.52 Oak hall robe with pictorial inlaid design. R1155

5.53 Detail 5.52

5.54 Detail 5.52

Chapter 6 Sources of Inspiration

So far we have looked at the history of Shapland and Petter, examined the factors which lay behind their commercial success and considered the decoration and construction of their pieces. Key questions which arise now are whether we can establish who designed the individual pieces of furniture. Was there an identifiable designer, a leading creative force or was the style created by an in-house team buying, borrowing and adapting designs from the market place in general? It seems from the evidence available that both of these questions can be answered positively.

The similarity of some pieces to designs of Baillie Scott, the influence of Voysey and of Ashbee can be clearly identified. Strong similarities exist between furniture produced by Liberty and by Shapland and Petter and many pieces have been attributed to Liberty which were made in Barnstaple. Its clear that a large number of retail companies bought furniture from Barnstaple which was sold under their own name, and this has given rise to speculation that known designers who worked for these companies may have created designs for Shapland and Petter to make up. However there appears to be very little evidence to support this view.

Taking a broader view of the development of Arts and Crafts in Barnstaple and North Devon at the turn of the century, it is interesting to consider what might have been the role of local factors in the design and techniques of decoration. Barnstaple had well established Art Potteries supplying London's West End through Liberty and by the early years of twentieth century members of Barnstaple School of Art, and the Guild of Metalworkers were commended frequently in *The Studio* and other art journals for creative design and skilled work.

However, whilst it is clear that a tradition of Arts and Crafts had been established in Barnstaple and any number of local people may have contributed to the design of furniture and its decoration, it does seem that there were key individuals such as Christopher Deubler, the marquetry specialist, and William Cowie, the designer who played very special roles in creating the Shapland and Petter style. Others such as James Rudd, another member of the Shapland and Petter design team also played an important part.

Lastly, it interesting to pose the question as to whether there was any direct involvement from the Shapland or the Petter families. Members of the families did work in the company but were they purely business orientated or were they involved in design to any extent? There is a little evidence which suggests that one family member, Henry Percy Shapland the grandson of the founder did provide some artistic influence in design and this will be considered in this chapter.

Arts and Crafts in Barnstaple

The craft tradition of Barnstaple included major involvement in lace making, art pottery and cabinet making. The establishment of the Literary and Scientific Institution in Barnstaple High Street in 1845 introduced a range of classes for the general improvement of the working classes, together with a library. By the 1860s, free art classes were added, taught by Alexander Lauder, owner of an Art Pottery in the town and these were attended by young designers from Brannam's Art Pottery and Shapland and Petter's craftsmen from the Raleigh Cabinet works studying design and woodcarving.

It is worth noting from the records of the Institution that a young student, William Lethaby scored high in architectural design in 1874. Lethaby, born in Barnstaple, became an important architect, furniture designer and a leading Arts and Crafts educationalist. Whilst he was most influential in design nationally no evidence has come to light to suggest that he had any involvement in the design of furniture by Shapland and Petter.

In 1877 the Institution moved to a new home in Barnstaple and became the North Devon Athenaeum, leaving the High Street premises to become established as the Barnstaple School of Art, the first municipally-owned School of Art in the country. Here the teaching of art and handicrafts was firmly established, with over 100 people attending by 1880. The *North Devon Journal* recorded the acquisition of premises for the School of Art, '*for the purposes of a school for the instruction of children and adults in drawing, painting, modelling and designing for architecture, manufacturing and decoration*'.[115] It is interesting to note here that Richard Arthur Shapland, son of the founder a key mover and shaker in the Shapland and Petter company was a member of the first committee responsible for the administration of the new School of Art.

As the School developed, modelling, moulding, design in textile fabrics, carving and furniture were on the curriculum. A note in the *North Devon Journal* mentions prizes awarded to Miss Petter for drawings and to Mr Cowie for '*designs for a suite of furniture and studies of historic styles of ornament which are carefully worked out*'. Cowie's drawings '*Art Catalogue*' and '*Decorative Design*' won

Best drawings by Artisans Prize and F.W. Petter won second prize for *Architectural Designs*.[116]

By 1894 the School of Art had established success rates amongst the highest for the country in government examinations managed through the Department of Science and Art at the South Kensington Museum. Efforts to inspire local people in the Arts and Crafts movement are evident in an article by Maud Partridge, based on a lecture given to the Barnstaple Reading Circle in 1900. In the article she echoes the views of Ruskin and Morris, criticising the manufacture of articles in wood by machine, questioning why a deal door should be grained to make it look like oak, a table of common wood veneered to make it look like mahogany, or coal boxes made to look too good to hold common coals. Clearly, she must have felt some antipathy to Shapland and Petter's 'state of the art' machine shops. Her closing paragraph is given in full:-

'The age of machinery, we will hope, is reaching or has reached its climax – and that the time is coming when we will rather have one hand-made thing showing the worker's thought in it, than that our rooms should be filled with things that a machine can turn out by the hundreds and that has degraded, instead of elevated, some fellow being in the making.'[117]

By the turn of the century the Arts and Crafts movement in Barnstaple started to make its presence felt in polite society as Fred Partridge (see below), his fiancée Miss Hart and others including Shapland and Petter lent their work and treasures for a Grand Art and Loan exhibition in aid of the North Devon Infirmary in Barnstaple.[118] The work of the artistic community in Barnstaple also began to be recognised in *The Studio*, e.g. 'honourable mention' given to Maud Partridge for a painting.[119]

In the early years, the School of Art was clearly a resource for training in technical as well as artistic skills and in 1892 the *North Devon Journal* noted that *'A numerously-signed requisition, endorsed by the employers, has been forwarded to the County Council by the men of Bridge Wharf Cabinet Works asking for the appointment of a Lecturer on Ornament and Design, particularly with reference to their own manufacturers. The memorial has been duly acknowledged and it is the nucleus of a permanent Students' Association and an educational benefit not only to the cabinet-makers themselves, but also to those engaged in the different potteries and kindred works in the neighbourhood.'*[120]

C.R. Ashbee

Shortly after the presentation of the request, C.R. Ashbee visited Barnstaple in 1893 as part of a programme of lectures and presented a twelve week course on 'Design as Applied to Furniture'. It is assumed that this was hosted by Shapland and

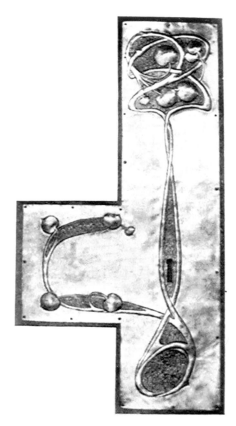

6.1 Metalwork by F. Braddon of the Barnstaple Guild of Metalworkers shown in The Studio 1902

Petter but whatever the employees thought of Ashbee, he was less than impressed with his hosts:-

'Plymouth Brethren v.godly and v.mean- and they will not do anything at all for education but look at it merely from the point of view of the market. On the whole the educational outlook for Barnstaple is about as bad as it can be.'[121]

There are no records to indicate what Ashbee might have tried to teach and one can only guess that his influence may have been to help the company move away from Victorian to the new Arts and Crafts style. At the time, in his own work at the Guild of Handicraft, Ashbee was designing 'joiners furniture' of heavy frame and panel construction with broad 'restful' surfaces . This style which he developed seems a reaction to the elaborate Victorian style with very 'busy' detail of bobbin turning, bevelled mirrors, glass shelves and little nooks and gilding. Ashbee's furniture was usually made in oak, basswood and walnut, sometimes green stained and either plain with period details stripped away, or decorated with painted design or coloured and gilded gesso. Ashbee designs which feature inlaid and painted decoration and elaborate metalwork did not appear until several years after his visit to Barnstaple. As he appeared not to have returned to Barnstaple after his visit it would seem unlikely that his influence on Shapland and Petter design extended beyond helping to create the genre for furniture design and decoration from which Shapland and Petter developed their own house style.

Art Metalwork and the Barnstaple Guild of Metalwork

Metalwork also featured in the curriculum for the School of Art with teaching in Arts and Crafts repoussé and enamelling skills. An article in *The British Architect* in 1901 featured Barnstaple School of Art[122] and illustrated repoussé metalwork by F. Braddon and J. Dewdeny who were both leading decorators at the Brannam Art Pottery, and a plaque with inset enamel panels by T. Charbonnier the principal of the School of Art. The Barnstaple Guild of Metalworkers, under the direction of G. Lloyd Morris came to the notice of *The Studio* which published an article featuring jewellery, silver and steel jewellery with brass and copper brooches by Fred Partridge, the Barnstaple born jeweller and former member of the Guild of Handicraft.[123]

In another reference to Barnstaple, *The Studio* congratulated itself for spreading the influence of Arts and Crafts from London to the humble provinces:-

'Barnstaple- The influence of The Studio is not confined to the large cities; even in a small town like Barnstaple it makes itself felt. It stands to the credit of North Devon that its metropolis, which has already a reputation for pottery is showing signs of life in metal-working and other crafts. A guild has now been formed which for the last nine months has been producing work of an interesting and varied character.'[124]

6.2 Detail of oak bureau with hand-beaten copper hinges and lock plate. R1529

The article describes work by Fred Partridge; *'A casket designed in brass and decorated with small enamels... the apex set with lapis stones.'* F. Braddon is also mentioned as exhibiting a copper doorplate with repoussé design in Celtic style. See 6.1. The hand-beaten hinges and lock plate shown in 6.2 are unusual and may have been made at the Guild of Metalwork.

Clearly there were cultural and educational resources in Barnstaple supporting and nurturing Arts and Crafts skills. Whilst little is known of links between Shapland and Petter and the School of Art or with the Guild of Metalwork it is a reasonable assumption that they must have been interlinked, mutually reinforcing developments in decorative arts and crafts. Evidence for this exists in the example of Indenture Papers for an apprentice cabinet maker who was required to sign an agreement that he would attend classes at the School of Art as part of his apprenticeship[125] and also the fact that Richard Arthur Shapland was a member of the committee for administering the School of Art.

In-House designers

From the ledgers which survive it is clear that a small team of designers were employed at the works on a regular salaried basis. The head of the design team in the period between the end of the nineteenth and early twentieth century was William Cowie who was the major creative designer for the company during the Arts and Crafts years. Others mentioned in the ledger are James Henry Rudd and the young grandson of the founder, Henry Percy Shapland, are also considered to have created designs and contributed to the house style during the period. Before discussion of individual designers, however it is important to look at the wider context from which inspiration and designs were gathered.

Bought in designs and books

As early as 1880 Shapland and Petter were noticed for their readiness to buy furniture designs. A survey for *The Cabinet Maker* notes that 'Barnstaple pays the best prices for designs'.[126] There does appear to have been a ready supply of designs on the market, regular features in *The Cabinet Maker* and *Furniture and Decoration* presented designs and drawings by staff designers. *The Studio* also ran competitions for design and illustrated prize-winning entries.

Two designers, Tims and Webb, were particularly prolific in the 'New Art Style' and became Art Directors of the *Furniture Record* in 1900. Their book *Thirty five Styles of Furniture* was recorded as a purchase by Shapland and Petter in 1904 for one pound and five shillings, along with other design books by Strange and French, Hoffman and others from Batsford and Co.[127] Other entries include *'Designs Das Interiors'* and *'Photographs from South Kensington'* and its clear that many sources of inspiration were drawn upon in the design room in Barnstaple.

Books used in the Shapland and Petter studio, to decorate items being photographed included *The Studio Year Book of Decorative Art, English Furniture* by G.M. Ellwood, *Collings Medieaval Foliage* and *Alphabets A Manual of Lettering* by E.F. Strange. It is interesting to note that a copy the *Tynecastle Tapestry* catalogue also appears in the photographs. This product range produced by Scott Morton and Co. produced Arts and Crafts inspired wall coverings, and were associated with Scottish Arts and Crafts architect George Lorimer. Tynecastle Tapestry designs of George and the Dragon are considered to have inspired Baillie Scott in the design for a fireplace.[128]

Scrap book of furniture styles

Whilst virtually no original drawings or documents from the design room were preserved for the archive, a fascinating insight into the style of working is given in the survival in the archive of large scrap books of pictures and cuttings of every conceivable European period style of furniture. Photographs include cuttings from *The Cabinet Maker* and *Country Life*. Pictures of a book case by Charles Rennie Mackintosh, a furnished room designed by Voysey and a writing cabinet by Baillie Scott are included in this bundle. Clearly, designers were able to borrow whole or part designs and copy details from a wide range of styles and individual pieces from this resource.

Influence of other companies

At the turn of the century Liberty appeared very much as the market leader for Arts and Crafts furniture and decorative arts, with their central position in Regent Street and their sophisticated marketing through catalogues and advertising. Heals, J.S. Henry, J.P. White, and Norman and Stacey among many others were selling Arts and Crafts furniture also in London, and in Glasgow, Wylie and Lochhead were predominant with smaller firms such as Pratts in Bradford, Goodall Heighway and Lamb in Manchester. Shapland and Petter appear to have done business with most of these companies (except Heals) but there is no evidence in the archives examined to suggest that they were making up designs from these companies' own designers or other well known national designers such as Baillie Scott or the Glasgow School designers associated with these companies.

Liberty and Co.

Many of the decorated Arts and Crafts pieces designed and made by Shapland and Petter have been attributed to Liberty. Examples include the firescreen and the bookcase illustrated 6.4.

The bookcase has been attributed to the Glasgow designer E.A. Taylor but without any clear reference to the evidence base.[129] Each of these pieces appear in the Shapland and Petter catalogue and/or archive and there can be little doubt that they were made in Barnstaple.

The L&C marking found on handles and hinges has been assumed by many to be the trade mark for Liberty and taken as evidence that the furniture bearing such handles was made or retailed by Liberty. This is not supported by evidence and the Author's own research at the Public Records Library confirmed in 2002 that L&C is the mark for Loach and Clarke, Art Metalworkers from Birmingham. Loach and Clarke were mentioned in the Shapland and Petter ledger as a supplier (see Chapter 5).

Attribution of Barnstaple pieces to Liberty seems often to be based simply on the assumption that the piece in question is in the 'Liberty Style'. The Shapland and Petter archive now provides the evidence base to force us to re-think the concept of Liberty Style. It clear that Shapland and Petter design and construction has been 'absorbed' into the general style of Liberty and when Shapland and Petter pieces are properly attributed this brings the credit back to Barnstaple and leaves the Liberty Style looking somewhat diminished.

6.3 Page from one of the scrap books of pictures Shapland and Petter archive showing Baillie Scott cabinet top left and centre right

2032
Extreme Width 3 ft. 10 in ; Height 5 ft 8 in.
Back, Bottom and Shelves Lined with Velveteen or Silk Tapestry.
Mahogany Inlaid with Pearl as shewn . . ~~£10 : 5 : 0~~

2032a £13 : 10 : 0
Sheraton Treatment. No Inlaid Pilaster between Upper Doors.
Back, Bottom and Shelves Lined with Velveteen or Silk Tapestry.
~~Wainscot Oak with Inlaid Fancy Lines~~ . . . ~~£10 : 17 : 6~~
Mahogany ,, £12 : 15 .: 0 ~~12 : 7 : 0~~
~~Greywood~~ ,, ,, . . . ~~13 : 10 : 0~~

6.4 Above High Class Furniture firescreen with peacock inlay. R2257, below
High Class Furniture bookcase with leaded lights. R2032

6.5 Photo archive. Hallstand with Liberty annotation

6.6 Oak overmantel with copper panels. R6006

Whilst there is some evidence that Shapland and Petter supplied Liberty, only three examples have been identified in the archive of photographs. The piece illustrated 6.5, a hall stand, is quite plain, others identified are not in Arts and Crafts style. Further support for the lack of a strong relationship between the two companies is that in all the furniture illustrated in Liberty catalogues from 1890 to 1920 there are no recognisable Shapland and Petter pieces. Unlike the catalogues of Wylie and Lochhead, Christopher Pratt or Norman and Stacey which show several examples of Shapland and Petter furniture, Liberty's catalogues show only one possible item which is the overmantel Illustrated 6.6. A similar version of this appears in the *Furniture for Town Flats and Country Houses* catalogue of Liberty.[130]

The other possible source of confusion in attribution may be the deliberate copying of designs. Whilst there are clear similarities in decoration; the stencilled landscapes and figures in panels for example, there appears to be only one glaring example of each company 'sharing' the same design. The Athelstan bedroom suite is illustrated as a drawing in the Liberty Archive Book of

Sketches, probably drawn by Leonard Wyburd circa 1898 and must have been a popular line for Liberty.[131] A surprisingly similar version is shown in the Shapland and Petter photo archive, without a date. This piece conforms in shape decoration to the Liberty piece and also has the same wooden handles. Apart from this however there appears to be little overlap between the two companies and the most feasible hypothesis at the moment seems to be that they were in competition, rather than in a relationship of strong collaboration or of commissioner and provider.

Named designers Benson, Napper and Baillie Scott

Whist there are no famous names recorded in the ledger as people paid for designs, there are occasional examples of pieces in the photo archive which are known as the work of other designers. The table labelled 'Morrish', (probably for Morris and Co) is a design attributed to W.A.S Benson, and the chair shown is known as a design by Harry Napper. It is feasible that Shapland and Petter did take commissions to make up designs, on

6.7 Photo archive. Wardrobe from a bedroom suite with stencilled design

occasion but there appears to be little evidence of this as a general practice, these being the only known examples.

Perhaps the most intriguing designs are those which bear some resemblance to the work of Baillie Scott. The most apparent similarity is in the mahogany display cabinet (Illustration 4.28) which was clearly a popular line for Shapland and Petter as several examples have been sold at auction in recent years. The inlaid design of lilies is very similar indeed to the cabinet by Baillie Scott. Shown 1.9. The structural shape of the cabinet however bears no resemblance to any of Baillie Scott's work and seems rather Victorian in shape rather than modern or new art. In the absence of any evidence to the contrary it would seem the design was simply copied from or inspired by Baillie Scott rather than being his own design for Shapland and Petter.

Of the other pieces for which resemblance to Baillie Scott's work is claimed, attributions can be traced back to the inlaid work on the settle made for J.P. White. See 6.10. Several authors, and sellers have followed the assumption that the dwarf bookcase and settle illustrated 6.14 are of Baillie Scott design, as are the bedroom suites and chairs which bear similar inlay of pewter ebony and other woods or mother of pearl.

6.8 Photo archive. Chair in the style of Harry Napper

6.9 Photo archive. Table in the style of W.A.S. Benson

6.10 M.H. Baillie Scott designed for J.P. White. High backed settle made from oak and inlaid with macassar ebony, cherry, chestnut and pewter.

No evidence is known to exist of any involvement of Baillie Scott in the design of these Shapland and Petter pieces and whilst the chairs, hall furniture and small cabinets do resemble his designs in decoration and possibly in structure no stronger association has been shown to exist.

Possible connections with Baillie Scott exist in so far as he did apparently design a house in Barnstaple (which was never built) and had other commissions in the area.[132] No records of any link with the company have been found to date. It is most probable that the work of Baillie Scott inspired many provincial designers who would have access to his work in *The Studio, The Builder* and other periodicals. The J.P. White catalogue was also available from 1901 and was promoted in trade journals. Shapland and Petter staff in London, could also have seen the Baillie Scott inlaid settle and other designs by taking a short walk from Berners Street in London to the J.P. White shop in Margaret Street, just around the corner.

The small settle in the *High Class Furniture* catalogue has also been attributed to Baillie Scott through the connection with Wylie and Lochhead who featured this in their catalogue 1902.[133] The chequered inlay on the chairs and settle is also reminiscent of the Baillie Scott style but clearly made in Barnstaple, without any apparent input from Baillie Scott. A chair and a stick stand are illustrated from the set of hall furniture most frequently attributed to Baillie Scott (4.41, 6.13) and the illustrated review article (3.24) published in 1903[134] features two

pieces from this set by Shapland and Petter. It is very pleasing to observe that the work of the craftsmen in Barnstaple could so readily have been accepted as the work of Baillie Scott, who was one of the most important furniture designers of the later Arts and Crafts period.

6.11 Oak dwarf bookcase with inlaid design. R900

Influence of Other designers

One fairly influential designer in the later years of the nineteenth century was C.H.B. Quennell. There is evidence that Quennell designed for Ambrose Heal and for J.P. White and initialled designs by him appear in *The Studio* and other periodicals.[135] The main feature of his design which appears in the work of Shapland and Petter is the heart pierced splat. This was used in many designs in different forms by Shapland and Petter and appears in published illustrations of beds by Heals and a garden bench for J.P. White apparently before being included in the Shapland and Petter repertoire.[136]

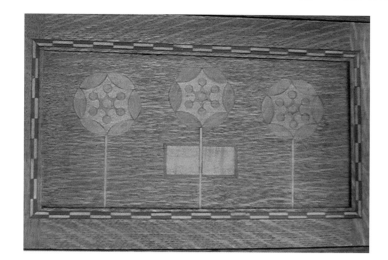

6.12 Oak dwarf bookcase with inlaid design. R901

6.13 Oak chair with inlaid design. R1089

6.14 High Class Furniture page of designs

William Cowie

The strongest and most consistent influence in the design of Shapland and Petter furniture was that of William Cowie, a Scotsman born in Stirling in 1858. Cowie moved to Barnstaple and studied at the Barnstaple School of Art as a young man. Little is known of the biography of Cowie and until 2005 the only known references to his association with the company were in the Shapland and Petter ledgers in which his pay as head of the design team was recorded.

However, early in 2005 a large, incomplete catalogue of drawings was discovered and subsequently acquired by the author for the Museum of Barnstaple and North Devon. Pages of the designs

have the inscription W. Cowie and sometimes 'Des' (for designer) following his name. An assessment of this catalogue suggests that these drawings are by the same hand and we can assume from this document that this was Cowie's master work, collating most of his designs and produced as a marketing catalogue.

In these designs we see some of the most powerful and charismatic pieces by Shapland and Petter, which have the defining characteristics of their style. The Hall robe with inlaid peacocks, the hall mirror, the buffet, bureau, bookcases and settles each have the classic structures and styles of decoration which are the essence of the Arts and Crafts style created by Shapland and Petter. Designs include the full range of decorative details inlaid ebony and pewter, repoussé copper panels with mottoes and

6.15 Oak wardrobe with inlaid design of pewter, abalone, coloured woods and inset enamels. R329

with ceramic and enamelled 'roundels' inset. There are fewer items with stencilled design shown than in the *High Class Furniture* photographic catalogue, and the finer cabinets and items with Baillie Scott influence are not represented. Designs featuring Glasgow roses patterns are also underrepresented.

The date of the catalogue has not been established. Whilst there are numerical annotations indicating 1910 on some pages it is not clear if these are dates of designs or subsequent notes. The catalogue of sketches does appear to include designs from an earlier date than the photographic version with a number of designs included which relate to the 'rabbit hutch' style

sideboards which were illustrated in 1894. See 1.11. There are also many pieces shown that are not Arts and Crafts in style and it would seem that Cowie also produced designs for the more traditional market as well as the new artistic movement.

What is known of William Cowie offers little insight into his development as an artist and designer or his relationships with other designers of the period. He appears in the 1891 census returns for Barnstaple as 'Furniture designer and draftsman'. In the 1901 census he is recorded as a 'Furniture Designer' 42 years old, living with his wife Anna and seven children, which included twin boys aged one year. Anna was German and her

6.16 Detail of 6.15

sister Louisa was Charles Petter's second wife (Charles was the son of Henry Petter, co founder of the firm). William Cowie was known to be a member of the Plymouth Brethren and lived in Ashleigh Road in Barnstaple, as did Deubler, the leading marquetry specialist.

It is clear that Cowie was the central figure in the design team and was paid a high salary for a designer. For example, records show that in 1894 he was paid £321 per annum, ten times more than most of the other members of the team. It is probable that he would have been paid additional fees for providing drawings for the hand-drawn catalogue which must have taken many months of work, and this may account for some large lump sum payments recorded in the ledgers. There are also recorded payments to G. Cowie for drawings, and this may well have been William's son Robert Gottfick, who would have been only 14 or 15 years old at the time, presumably copying drawings rather than creating original designs.

Henry Percival Shapland

Henry Percival Shapland was the son of William Henry Shapland and grandson of Henry, the founder. He was born in 1880, destined to become a leading authority on furniture history and design in the early part of the twentieth century. The young Henry recorded in the ledgers as 'P. Shapland' spent a brief period in the design team and was paid £25. 5. 0. in 1898, but only 10 shillings in 1899, after which he is believed to have left, as he is not mentioned again.

Percy was registered with the Royal Institute of British Architects as a qualified architect, who was articled to Charles Edward Varndell in Surrey. He must have left Barnstaple in his late twenties as he is known to have lived in Cannonbury Square in London from 1909 to 1914. His career in architecture seem to have been short lived as he was clearly passionately interested in furniture with an early publication on *Style Schemes* in 1909[137] and by 1926 he was editor of the Cabinet Maker and Cantor Lecturer at the Royal Society of Arts. His best known work was the *Practical Decoration of Furniture,*[138] which, in three volumes, is a scholarly and comprehensive work. He wrote several other books and introductions for studies of furniture. Unfortunately he seems to have had only a fleeting interest in Arts and Crafts design as there are virtually no references to the movement or to the Shapland and Petter contribution to artistic furniture in any of his works identified to date.

Much more research is needed to understand his role in the development of the Shapland and Petter style. Clearly, he had an artistic flair and a published drawing signed by him shows very typical decorative inlaid design with five vertical bracts and small Lily pad leaves. See 6.22. A series of drawings published in the *Furniture Record* in 1901 are signed HPS with the initial S very similar to that in his full signature.[139] These drawings show cabinets with copper grilles in plant forms which are classic Shapland and Petter designs. The handles drawn are identical to those on the fire surround and it is assumed these designs were by H.P. Shapland, who was then twenty-one years old.

There are interesting similarities between these drawings and cabinets made by Shapland and Petter but the most striking cross reference is the plant forms on the cabinet designs marked HPS and the design on the covers of the Shapland and Petter Catalogues (Illustrated Chapter 3). The familiar pattern of 5 vertical leaves and stems seems almost from the same hand. Another interesting piece of evidence from the catalogue for *China Cabinets* is the Glasgow style rose design which bears the initial HS in stylised form which could also be his initials.

The style of drawing of H.P. Shapland, is slightly more sparse and less florid than Cowie, the lines seem more attenuated and

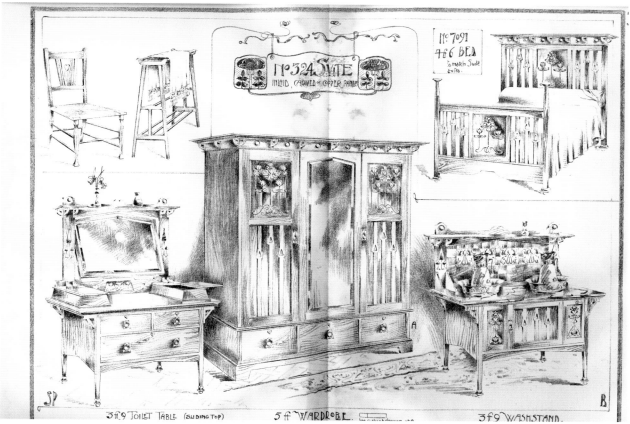

6.17 Catalogue of Drawings. Bedroom suite 324

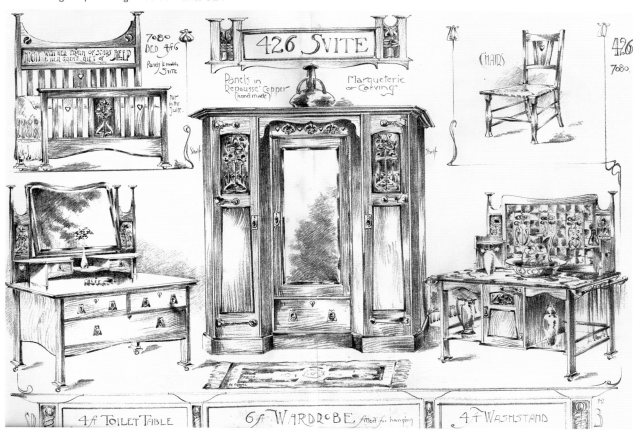

6.18 Catalogue of Drawings. Suite R426.

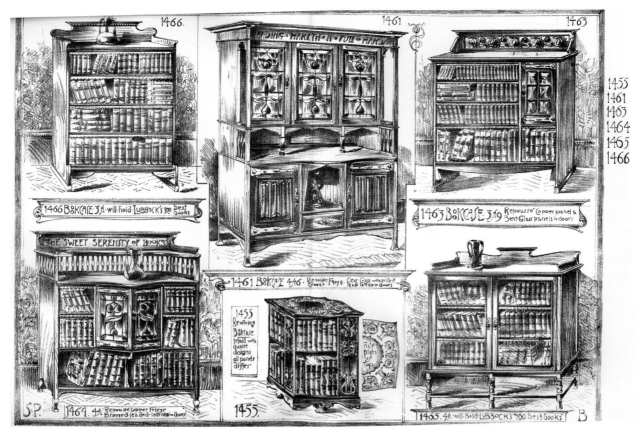

6.19 Catalogue of Drawings. Bookcases

6.20 Catalogue of Drawings. Sideboards and buffets signed William Cowie

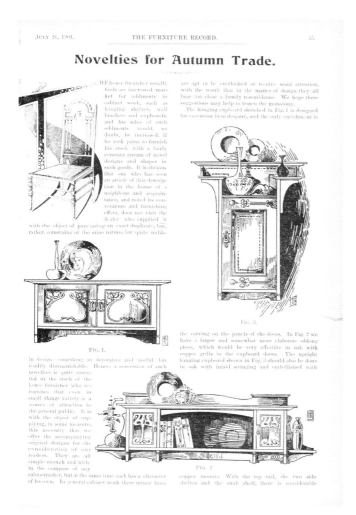

6.21 Designs for Cabinets marked HPS. Furniture Record July 1901

6.22 H.P. Shapland Design for an inlaid chimney piece

6.23 Signature and monograms: H.P. Shapland

perhaps influenced by the sinuous style of Art Nouveau. His vision may well have influenced the decorative inlays and marquetry work in the early 1900s and there are examples of decoration which do appear to follow his line. Overall, the artistic input of H.P. Shapland appears very small compared to the powerful and comprehensive influence of William Cowie but it is essential to research more rigorously to understand his role.

James Henry Rudd

Another in-house designer who worked at Shapland and Petter for some years was James Rudd. He was an employee of the company who drifted from the bench to the drawing office and from there to the art and technical schools taking South Kensington examinations. Two books written by him on furniture making have been identified but neither has significant Arts and Crafts references.[140] An article about him in the *North Devon Journal* in 1919 described his work as a designer in furniture and his commendation from William Lethaby for his capability in the art of design.[141] His designs for Pilkingtons tiles and for metalwork are mentioned and his success at Arts and Crafts exhibitions in Paris and St Louis also cited.

Rudd is included in a special feature by *The Studio* in 1909 identifying the leading European Designers and Craftsmen.[142] His work designing tiles for Godwin and Hewit is presented and reference made to his exhibits at the Arts and Crafts Society Exhibition in London. Here is another exciting possibility for research as very little information about Rudd or his contribution to Shapland and Petter designs has been identified. The tiles illustrated do have a definite affinity with Shapland and Petter designs, (see for example tiles on the White Bedroom Suite in Glasgow style illustrated 4.27) and it is important to try to establish more about his work.

Christopher William Deubler

In an examination of design and inspiration the last word should be for Christopher William Deubler, the German master craftsman and artist who is assumed to have created the Shapland and Petter pictorial designs executed in marquetry and intarsia. As with William Cowie and H.P. Shapland little information exists on this central character. It is know that he was German, a member of the Plymouth Brethren and was a

TILES DESIGNED BY J. H. RUDD, EXE-
CUTED BY GODWIN AND HEWITT

6.24 Tiles designed by J.H. Rudd. The Studio 1909

highly paid freelance craftsman. The lack of information leaves one to assume that he drew and then cut the pictorial designs and whilst in many we see Cowie's hand, in others there is a distinct 'continental' feel e.g. the panel illustrated 6.25 shows buildings which appear to be German or Austrian in character. Deubler when free to design to his own taste may have brought a different perspective to the new art which must at times have seemed suffocating with endless floral and repetitive patterns of peacocks and matrix designs.

The picture panels which he created have warmth and subtlety, perspective and superb colour balance which improves with age and gentle care. These creations provide depth and authority to the pieces of furniture which they decorate, giving them real beauty as decorative pieces and a true status as ' blossoms of the art of furniture'.

6.25 Detail of inlaid panel from oak bureau. R1529

6.26 Oak hall robe with inlaid panels and hand-wrought copper work. R1371

6.27 Oak wardrobe with inset enamel discs and inlaid panels. Suite R429

6.28 Detail of 6.26

6.29 Detail of 6.27

6.30 Detail of dressing table for suite shown 6.15

Chapter 7 Collecting Shapland and Petter Furniture

7.1 Shapland and Petter and Raleigh Labels.

This chapter deals with the identification of Shapland and Petter furniture and looks at the archive information which relates to the design numbers, labels and trade marks of the company. The aim is to answer some very basic questions on recognising Shapland and Petter pieces and the trade marks associated with the company.

For the serious collector or for those who might simply wish to have just one or two pieces, the range produced by Shapland and Petter provides the ideal opportunity for investment and lasting pleasure. A precondition for establishing a broad base of collectors is that there must be a large number of pieces in circulation or potentially available. The enormous range of pieces produced by Shapland and Petter and their very wide geographical distribution networks create exciting prospects for collectors. There has been a steady trickle of original and previously unseen pieces coming onto the market in recent years.

The fact that so much Shapland and Petter furniture has survived suggests that it has been useful, well made and good to live with,

surviving two world wars and, the greater perils of the 1960s when many antiques of this period were 'modernised', painted orange and purple or ended up in a skip. Looking at surviving pieces today shows they benefit from the most robust construction and in handling these pieces one is reassured by their weight and solidity compared to some examples of modern furniture.

Of those pieces which survive, most are recognised and highly prized by collectors but there are others gently slumbering unrecognised either for their market value or their origins in Barnstaple and these trickle onto the auction market when owners circumstances or preferences change. There is no record of how many pieces were produced but it is clear that much of the furniture they produced has survived presumably as it has been revered and respected or perhaps just tolerated as it performed a useful function. Certainly the quality of the woods used and the craftsmanship in design, machining and construction have given Shapland and Petter pieces a strong chance of long life.

The archive material, which is still growing as new items come to light, gives a unique overview of the range of pieces but also indicates the possibility of endless variations on decorative and structural characteristics. From the catalogues, we know that customers could choose between copper panels or inlaid or carved work in many cases, and consequently a great variety of pieces has been observed, with different versions and occasional examples of customised pieces.

Another important factor in collecting is that the method of attribution should be as definite and accessible as possible so we can be sure that we are collecting the genuine article and confident of the integrity of the piece. Collecting Leica cameras and Leitz accessories for example is a more certain activity because of the extensive and precise database, whereas collecting Arts and Crafts furniture does not reach the same level of certainty. Optimistic and profit based attribution of pieces such as 'almost certainly Liberty and Co' or 'attributed to Liberty' without any evidence in support of the claim have become commonplace particularly in web trading and this may in fact erode confidence in the market for new collectors.

For collectors of Shapland and Petter, there are now much stronger grounds upon which attribution can be made and a more coherent picture of their house style is emerging. This is in contrast to Liberty for example, where a wide range of pieces of variable quality and design were supplied from different companies, (including Liberty's own workshops) and then given the Liberty label. Shapland and Petter furniture was all made in Barnstaple[143] and each has a clear provenance which can be verified. This must certainly help to increase confidence in this field of collecting.

Evidence-based attribution

By now most readers will recognise the Shapland and Petter style without very much difficulty, being able to attribute pieces according to those structural characteristics, and decorative designs which were very much exclusive to Shapland and Petter. However, experienced based or intuitive recognition has been much exploited within the business of selling Arts and Crafts pieces. Many pieces of Shapland and Petter have been attributed to Liberty, Wylie and Lochhead and other companies and so the credit for design and skill in manufacture has not been attributed to Barnstaple, where it belongs.

Fortunately, the discovery of catalogues in addition to the archives at Barnstaple has created a much greater database of illustrated and numbered designs which is now probably the largest data base of any in the Arts and Crafts field. The database which is still developing opens up a whole new perspective on collecting Arts and Crafts as it provides the opportunity for evidence- based attribution.

Labels

The most obvious place to look for identification is on a label and whilst many pieces of Shapland and Petter have labels attached, invariably these are for retailers who were supplied with furniture by Shapland and Petter. Figure 1 lists some of the many companies represented in ledgers and examples of some of the different retailer's labels observed.

Shapland and Petter labels are extremely rare, only six examples have been identified by the author to date and these are shown in 7.1. Only one example of each has been found so far.

Figure 1 Furnishing Companies, Department Stores, and Customers of Shapland and Petter

Names in the Archives; some examples	Names in the Ledgers	Labels applied to furniture
Guest & Wardle, Waring & Gillow, Hudson & Hepper, Kendal-Milne, Whiteley Ltd, Smith & Co, Gardner, Hayward, Toomer, Cole Bros, Hamptons, Cohen, General Shipping Co., Craig, Clarabut, Pedlar, Goodall, Jones & Son, London County Council. M J & C. (Marsh Jones and Crib?), Bath Cabinet Co, Williams & Cox, Glazer (Glaser), Liberty, Miller & Beatty, McKendrick, Boulting, Malcolm, Mappin & Webb, Chinnery, Liver Co, Mitchell & Guttering, Garlick Ltd, Fieldhouse Bridgeman of Torquay, Burton and Son. Messrs Tapling and Co. Morrish, Shoolbred. Wylie and Lochhead	Pratts of Bradford Goodall Lamb and Heighway, Warings, Norman and Stacey, Wylie and Lochead	Jenners Edinburgh Jones and Higgins. London. Story and Triggs. London Morgans

7.2 Jones and Higgins retailer's label on oak bedside cupboard

Raleigh

The Raleigh trade mark was used for several stamps and letterheads of the firm and an example of the stamped mark is shown. This emblem showing Sir Walter Raleigh, the Sixteenth century explorer, was not chosen at random as the company figurehead. The Raleigh family came to England with William the Conqueror and settled in Barnstaple a thousand years ago, giving their name to the manor of Raleigh, where Henry Shapland established his first workshop in the 1850s, using the medieval water mill to power his machinery. Sir Walter, born in East Devon, was descended from a branch of the Barnstaple family and Henry Shapland was perhaps pleased to connect his enterprise with that of the Elizabethan adventurer.[144] For a period the company used 'Raleigh' as the name for a range of items such as 'The Raleigh' Coal Boxes and also in conjunction with the initials S.P. or S.P-B. The term Registered Raleigh was also used, sometimes in conjunction with registered design numbers, though there appears to be only one example of this.

S&P-B Monograms and Marks

By far the most common mark for Shapland and Petter is the impressed stamp of S&P B in a triangular shape on locks. There are no known examples of this stamp on other parts of the metalwork or wood, as far as the author is aware, the mark appears only on the brass locks fitted to furniture. Whilst this mark makes attribution fairly straightforward, there are numerous examples of unmarked locks and the possible reasons for this include:-

- Small locks on cabinets and smokers cabinets are often unmarked.

- New locks have been put on by owners, where none were intended in the design.

- Locks have been changed during the last 100 years because of lost keys.

- Locks have been removed to 'enhance' other pieces of furniture.

- Locks were not stamped at the works.

7.3 Raleigh badge mounted on Shapland and Petter lorry circa 1920.

7.4 Raleigh Stamped mark. Archive Documents

7.5 Shapland and Petter monograms from catalogues. See Chapter 3.

In the case of the latter, locks for the more elaborate pieces, which are combined with handles to turn the latch, i.e. for hall robes and wardrobes have been observed to be unmarked. No apparent reason for this exists, but one could speculate that they were missed, or deliberately left unmarked at the instruction of the customer or retailer.

Monograms

S.P-B is the monogram for Shapland and Petter of Barnstaple and in some cases this was used on catalogues rather than the full name of the company. Searching library data bases or book sellers for Shapland and Petter may fail to identify original material filed under SPB as was the case with the National Art Library Catalogues in 2004. (See Chapter 3). Catalogues which have been found to date have the monogram on most pages, which is useful if fragments or single pages of catalogues are discovered.

The graphic presentation of this monogram varies, as shown in the illustrations. The bedroom furniture version 3.9 has a

similarity in style to the J.P. White and Baillie Scott monogram with linking of the letters.[145] No examples of this monogram have been identified on furniture or metalwork, or anything other than advertising material.

Stamped Numbers; Registered Designs. Rd numbers

A number of companies stamped identification on furniture which they made. Gillow, Waring and Gillow, Heal and sons, Liberty for example, frequently stamped the company name and companies such as Harris Lebus Ltd stamped HLL often marked with a Registered Design Number which is traceable through the Public Records Office at Kew in London.

Whilst there are several entries in the Shapland and Petter cash book around 1900 and 1902 for registration of designs, to date only two pieces of furniture produced by Shapland and Petter have been found to bear registration numbers, the hall seat illustrated 3.29 and a music cabinet.

Other design registrations have been identified as shown below. These are early registrations and are not for Arts and Crafts

7.6 Stamped mark S&PB the identification for Shapland and Petter

pieces though the bedroom suite does have aspects of aesthetic style and a similar version is illustrated in the catalogue of drawings.

Shapland and Petter Registered designs

199915,/8	1894	Coal Vases and Coal box
232535	1894	Palm Holder
241158	1894	Bedroom suite

Stamped Registration Numbers

A fairly reliable method for identification is to check for numbers impressed on the back of furniture. These numbers are often preceded by the letter R, but not always and are sometimes difficult to spot, unless the piece can be very closely

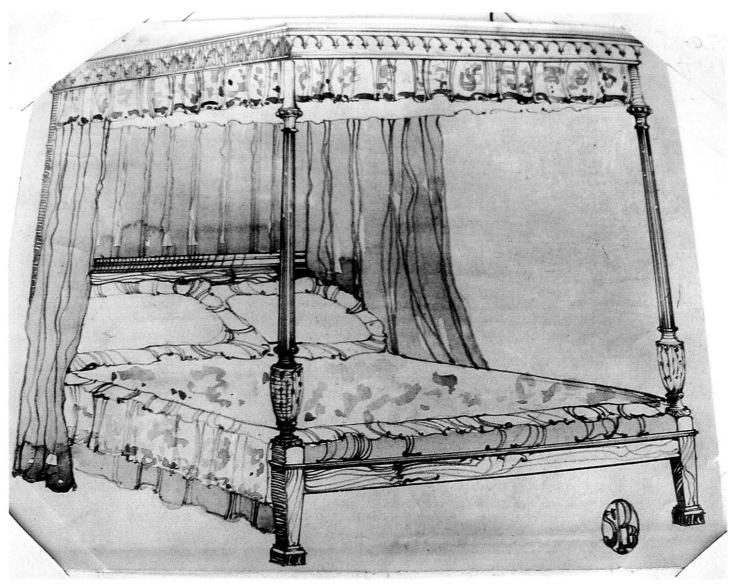

7.7 Drawing for a bed with monogram. Shapland and Petter archive

7.8 Registration Number impressed mark

examined from different angles. Characters which are stamped tend to conform to the size of R at 13 mm high and numbers at 9 mm high or 8mm on smaller pieces. Numbers are stamped individually, not as a group and spacing depth etc varies, in some cases numbers are arranged with four then three below or spaced in a block away from the first four. Numbers have also been observed handwritten in blue pencil or black pencil on small tables, and on the reverse of wooden panels which support inset copper panels from the back.

The meaning ascribed to these numbers is that the first four (or less) relate to the design, registered within the records of the company, and the other numbers are the individual numbering of pieces made to that design though they may relate to the page number of the design book. The numbers do not relate to the Register of Designs which are at the Public Records Office.

Registration Numbers observed

There are five main sources of information relating to the Registration numbers:

• The *Fine Furniture* Catalogues.
• The Catalogue of Drawings.
• The Photo archive.
• The numbered hand written sheets within the archive.
• Numbering observed on surviving pieces.

It is not surprising that these sources do not all match up in a completely reliable manner. Whilst record keeping and marking must have been considerably more rigorous than in many other companies, no single set data exists in the Shapland and Petter archive or elsewhere which encompasses all known numbers and designs.

Notwithstanding the lack of precision in numbering, broad guidelines to numbering schemes are shown in Fig. 2. It is very

important however to note that this is not a systematic collation of the numbers as there are many examples of items out of sequence, large gaps and later items included with significantly different numbers to the expected range.

As an indication of the lack of consistency across the different sources of information now available, fig 3 shows the results of a brief review of numbering for some specific pieces. The lack of consistency shows clearly that the process of stamping and numbering was not absolutely rigorous and catalogues showed only a selection of items available. The collection of archived photographs is incomplete with significant gaps e.g. there are no books of photographs for sideboards, hopefully some of the 'lost' records may be discovered or become available in time.

Attributed and 'Unofficial' Pieces

Given the information which has survived, the task of verification of pieces which at first seemed simply a matter of checking locks or R numbers, begins to look more complex, the more data we have. In the main however attribution on the basis of at least one

Figure 2 Broad guidelines for R Numbers Shapland and Petter

Fire Surrounds	90 to 252
Tea Wagons	1835 to 1838
Wall Cabinets, smokers cupboard	814 to 932
Sideboards	1874 to 1978, 1980 to 1985
Buffets	2000 to 2145
Overmantels	6006 to 6027
Revolving bookcases, bookstands, desks writing tables Some further items	1400 to 1560 2426 2562
China Cabinets	2022 to 2527
Occasional Tables	2078 to 2305
Hall Stands	999 to 1400 plus 2700 to 8
Hall Chairs	1036 to 1408
Coal Vases	1908 1994
Bedroom Suites	88 to 464
Beds	7000 to 7179

7.9 Hanging plaque with inlaid Glasgow rose design

characteristic i.e. the appearance in one database or a company mark is usually possible. In the absence of any such characteristic, the claim to be Shapland and Petter may be advanced on the basis of structural or decorative techniques and each case must be judged on its merits in respect to the known pieces and the data we have. As ever the maxim 'let the buyer beware' applies and one would hope that the optimistic dealer who 'attributes' on even the most remote similarity may rise to the challenge of a more evidence based approach.

An intriguing area for research is the probability of unofficial pieces made by employees of the company either as apprentice pieces which were not sold on the market or simply by home working, as a hobby. Given that there were hundreds of employees at Shapland and Petter at the turn of the century there is a strong probability that some would have used the techniques and possibly some waste or salvaged materials from the Raleigh Works. An example shown is the plaque with inlaid Glasgow roses which was bought at Pannier Market in Barnstaple. This piece is a genuine and original constructions and presumably the result of home working by employees. Other pieces with Shapland and Petter features specifically the geometric arch also have been observed.

Customised pieces

Caution is required in identifying custom made pieces i.e. those made not from an 'in house' design but made specifically to customer requirements. Whilst there was obviously a great deal of bespoke work in the shop fitting and joinery work for offices or municipal buildings, and churches, there appears to be no evidence of Arts and Crafts style work (with the possible exception of the Dutch style interior Chapter 3).

Figure 3 Stamped Registration numbers and other sources of evidence.

Item R Number	Illustration	Stamped locks	Photo Archive	Fine Furniture Catalogues	Catalogue of Drawings	Archive List hand written design numbers
Chair 1150	5.6	Na	Yes	Yes	Yes	-
Hall Table 1072	5.19	Na	-	Yes	Yes	-
Hall Mirror 1406	4.17	Na	-	-	Yes	-
Hall Table 1407	5.7	Na	-	Yes	Yes	-
Hall Robe 1176	4.20	Yes	Yes	Yes	-	-
Stick Stand 1035	5.37	Na	-	-	Yes	-
Hall Cupboard Peacocks 1399	4.18	Yes	-	-	Yes	-
Hall seat 1146	5.4	Na	-	-	Yes	-
Hall Robe	1.15	Yes	-	-	-	-
Wardrobe Glasgow Style 214 427	4.27	Yes	-	-	-	-
Bookcase painted panel 1541	4.13	Yes	-	Yes	-	-
Overmantle copper 6006	6.6	Na	-	Yes	Yes	-
Overmantel painted 6017	4.14	Na	-	Yes	-	-
Wall Cupboard 845	5.17	Yes	Yes	Yes	Yes	Yes
Sideboard 2165	5.26	Yes	-	-	-	-
Mahogany Display Cabinet	4.28	Yes	-	-	-	-
Hall Cupboard. Inlaid 1317	6.27	No	Yes	Yes	-	-
Display Cabinet 2027	3.18	Yes	Yes	Yes	-	Yes

The best is yet to come

The research carried out so far has been rewarding as much new evidence has been gathered and this has made it possible to assess the archive material in Barnstaple in a new light. Comparing and contrasting records and checking with existing pieces has strengthened the knowledge base on this important period of the company history. Whilst much more research is needed, the wealth of images now available and the certainty that there are still many more original pieces as yet undiscovered makes this one of the most exciting areas of collecting. Hopefully, the developing evidence base on the work Shapland and Petter will strengthen confidence and enjoyment in collecting their pieces and add to the knowledge base on the British Arts and Crafts movement.

7.10 Oak hall chair with peacock feather inlaid design. R1408

End notes

1   Wilson A.N. p139.

2   Morris.W Lecture; The Lesser Arts of Life 1878.

3   Eastlake C.L. p47.

4   Crane.W Of the Revival of Design and Handicraft in Arts and Crafts Essays, p12.

5   Calloway. S. p9,

6   White. JP Catalogue 1901 p4,

7   Furniture and Decoration 1894 Shapland and Petter New Designs Nov p143.

8   Furniture and Decoration & the Furniture Gazette October 1894 Recent Trade Literature p151,

9   Strong. R.1999 p521,

10 Forty. A. 1986 p72,

11 Ibid p101,

12 Ruskin. J.1853 p204,

13 Aslin. E.1962. p24,

14 Agius. P 1978. p153.

15 Building News vol. 14, 1867. p222,

16 North Devon Journal June 13 1872. p5,

17 Strong. H.W. 1889

18 Ibid p177,

19 One particularly serious fire occurred at the warehouse belonging to Wylie & Lochhead, upholsterers and undertakers at 43-47 Buchanan Street, was observed by thousands of Glaswegians making their way into the city centre on the night of Saturday 3 November 1883. The Wylie & Lochhead blaze was one of Victorian Glasgow's worst, causing damage worth over £200,000. Fires in the cabinet trade were reported regularly in The Furniture Record which, at the turn of the century ran a regular feature on Recent Fires.

20 Strong. H.W. p178.

21 Ibid p182.

22 Ibid p181.

23 Ibid.

24 Ibid p180 to 190.

25 Shapland.H.P.1926 p23.

26 Strong.H.W. p191.

27 Ibid p193.

28 Ibid.

29 Morris.W. 1948 p653.

30 Ashbee.C.R. Craftsmanship In Competitive Industry.nd p53.

31 Edwards. C 1993.

32 The Leaderflush Shapland company part of the LS Group formerly Shapland and Petter, still has a manufacturing base in Barnstaple.

33 Edwards. C 1993

34 Morris. W. Quoted in Lethaby. W.R. 1935 p94.

35 Ashbee Memoirs, Unpublished Typescript, 1938 V and A Library.

36 The discussion of the relationship between Shapland and Petter, Brethren and the Arts and Crafts movement in this chapter has been contributed by Dr Roger Shuff. For further reading see, F.R. Coad, A History of the Brethren Movement (Vancouver: Regent College, 2001); R. Shuff, Searching for the True Church (Carlisle: Paternoster, 2004).

37 Shapland. E Those were the days. The Cabinet Maker and Complete house furnisher Sept 29 1945 p305.

38 Aslin. E. 1962 p22.

39 The Furniture Gazette Oct 15 1891 p143.

40 Copyright in Furniture Trade Catalogues; An Important Case. Oetzmann versus Lefvrer The Furniture Record. Nov 15 1901.

41 Shapland E. p307.

42 Ibid.

43 National Art Library. SP-B Trade Catalogues TC.C Box 4.

44 The Furniture Record. Mssrs Shapland & Petter Ltd. 1905 p741.

45 The Furniture Record. Sept 26 1902 p310.

46 Strong. H.W. p177 'One circumstance which heightened the extent of the calamity was that the manufactured stock was abnormally large, to the tune of many thousand pounds, in consequence of the spring orders having been prepared for delivery in April'.

47 Williams.R 1998 p65.

48 Ibid p67.

49 The Furniture Record Sept 20 1901.

50 Wylie and Lochhead, 1902.

51 There was a significant increase in the retail price index during the first few years of the twentieth century.

52 White. J.P. 1901.

53 The Studio Yearbook. 1906.

54 The Furniture Record Oct 1901 p300.

55 Shapland E Ibid.

56 Ibid.

57 Furniture and Decoration 1894 p144.

58 Gardiner. W.F. 1897.

59 Harvey C. and Press J.1991

60 The Furniture Record Oct 13 1905 p467.

61 Ibid p506.

62 The Furniture Record Oct 20 1905 p742.

63 The Furniture Record 1902 Nov 28 p547and 548.

64 The Liberty Archives.Early Piracies 1932 Box 19/20 Liberty archive contains two large box files of correspondence for 'Piracy' where other companies used the word Liberty in connection with their own products or appeared to have copied designs. Liberty appear to have been very proactive in putting forward

Oak hall stand with copper panels

and protecting their brand name and there are example of companies, hoping to win favour, writing to Liberty to report infringements by local firms.

65 The tile illustrated was one of four salvaged from a hallstand which was considered beyond use. The author obtained in 2004 the tile directly from the person who reclaimed it in 2002.

66 Hilliard E. 1993 and also The Studio Vol 25 1901. p185.

67 See fig 1.

68 C.F.A. Voysey in Furniture and Decoration. Nov 1893 p167.

69 Gleeson White Some Glasgow Designers and their work The Studio Vol 11 1897 p89.

70 Talwin Morris The Studio Vol. 21 1902 p59.

71 The Furniture Record 1903 April 17 p421.

72 Baillie Scott designed and named the 'Carnation Lily, Lily Rose Cabinet' with inlaid white lilies which featured in the J.P. White Catalogue of 1901. The was presumably inspired for the painting Carnation Lily, Lily Rose by John Singer Sargant painted in 1885-6. This painting of children with paper lanterns and lilies was shown in The Studio Magazine in 1897 in the same volume as Baillie Scott's article on Small Country Houses. Baillie Scott also used the design in virtually the same shape and positioning in his design for a Music Cabinet illustrated in The Studio July 1898. see also A Small Country House Studio December 1897 p 167 to 177. and Some Furniture for the New Palace at Darmstadt. The Studio July 1898 p 91 to 97. Fabric designs also featured the Lily, Lindsay Butterfield's Tiger Lily design was sold from Heals from 1898 being a particularly vivid example. See Parry. L 1988.

73 M.H. Baillie Scott The Studio March 1899.

74 J.P. White 1901.

75 The tiles are not marked but are identical to a larger tile panel of the Medmenham Pottery shown at AFE Fairs Earls Court by Rue Miry August 2002 and are attributed on that basis. See also The Artist Sept/Dec 1902 p171, see note 104.

76 The Art of the Modern School Harry S Curry. The Artist May/Aug 1901 p203.

77 Helland. J 1996.

78 A card advertising a Short List of Books by BT Batsford found in the of the company archive included titles such as Alphabets old and New. Lewis F Day.

79 Gameson. R. 1997. Liberty also used this V in the Motto in their design for a bedroom which was shown in the window of their Regents Street Shop in 1897(see Parry L 1988 115) As with so many devices used in Arts and Crafts design the visual cues suggesting the item had originated in a bygone age were never far away.

80 M.H.Baillie Scott The Building News August 30, and May 10 1895 and The Studio October 1896.

81 C.F.A. Voysey in The British Architect January 1895.

82 Hitchmough.W. 1995 p62.

83 Lethaby W.R. 1891.

84 Shapland and Petter SPB The Raleigh Coal Boxes circa 1906 NAL.

85 Brown oak is English white oak that turns a deep brown colour from a fungal attack that brings about chemical change to the tree. This wood has a darker more dense figuring of cross grain

Fig 1. Some Plant forms used in Shapland and Petter Designs

Plant	Constructed	Has been observed
Honesty seed pods	Inlaid design in mother of pearl, occasionally with ebony and pewter. Rarely in repoussé copper.	Bedroom furniture, music cabinet, desk, smokers cabinet, overmantel
Glasgow rose	Widely used design Inlaid with shell and mother of pearl, ornamental woods and repoussé copper, also carved	Bedroom furniture, firescreen, overmantel, display and smokers cabinets, settle,
Tudor rose, briar rose and leaf	Rarely used	Mahogany bureau with motto 1529
Tulip	Commonly used in stylised form as bud and open flower inlay and repoussé copper	Overmantle, bed, firescreen, and variety of stylised forms
Lily flower stem and root	Inlaid with shell and mother of pearl, ornamental woods	In finest cabinets, in variety of panels
Water lily or lotus bursting fruit, exposed seeds. Closed buds	Inlay, repoussé copper; water lily leaves in hinges and lock plates. Lotus flower inlaid shell and mother of pearl	Wide variety of copper panels for hall and library furniture, finer inlay for display cabinets, music cabinet
Thistle	Inlaid and in repoussé	Hall mirror and hall furniture
Poppy	Occasional in repoussé copper	Sideboard. bed with motto
Plum/apple tree/tree of life	Carved and repoussé copper	Hall furniture
Daffodil	Inlaid design	Rare bookcase, smokers cabinet
Acanthus	Inlaid in Gothic style, combined with Glasgow rose or other plant forms	Display cabinets

and the figure and colour was said to be unrivalled. Being more difficult to work needing a longer time for seasoning increased the cost of this very special wood. Indications are that this was used more for the Victorian and Revivalist style pieces rather than the new 'artistic' range.

86 Lister Sutcliffe, G 1905.

87 Crawford. A. 1985 p284.

88 The Furniture Record. Artistic and High Class Furniture 1904 p174 .

89 Lister Sutcliffe, G 1905 Vol 2 p179. See also American definition and spelling 'Therming' Dwight. W. 1899.

90 See for example. The Artist 1897 and the Art Workers Quarterly 1889/90 p313.

91 The Furniture Record New Ideas in Inlaid work. Sept 15 1899. p146.

92 Illustration 5.10 centre top row, Impressed mark RD 232428 registered to Crofts and Assinder, Standard Works, Birmingham, Brass founders. 18 May 1894. (Traced by Dr Roger Shuff from registration design number identified by the author).

93 Raleigh SP-B Trade Catalogues TC.C Box 4 Raleigh High Class Modern Coal Boxes.

94 The Furniture Record. Oct 23 1901 p366.

95 Copper repoussé work articles appeared in The Studio, Vol 20 p86, John Williams formerly of the Guild of Handicraft published an article describing the techniques of repoussé work in The Art

Workers Quarterly 1905 p 38 and earlier article in Art Workers Quarterly 1903 Vol p 133 featured the Barnstaple School of Metalworking linked to School of Arts, established by G. Lloyd Morris. See also British Architect 1901 Dec 20 p 440. which featured items by the Barnstaple Guild of Metalworkers including a copper plaque with enamel roundels inset, by T Charbonnier Head of the School.

96 The Furniture Record April 17 1903 p421.

97 The Furniture Record 1905 June 30 p741.

98 Raleigh SP-B Trade Catalogues TC.C Box 4 Raleigh High Class Modern Coal Boxes

99 The Studio Vol 12 1897 p31.

100 The Studio Vol 16 1898 p108.

101 The Furniture Record April 17 1903 p421.

102 The Furniture Record June 30 1905 p741. An examination of the red enamel centre of the lock plate for the sideboard illustrated 5.26 showed a simple hand cut copper disc hammered into convex shape and then covered with a red enamel. The most simple technique yet in the centre of this restrained oak pieces it provides an exciting focal point There are also examples of enamel applied to hinges, a clock case illustrated in the photo archive shows these and a surviving example of this piece showed peacock blue enamels on the hinges and lock plate. A Smokers Cabinet was advertised by Shapland and Petter in High Class Furniture which featured enamels if requested, the catalogue offered Smokers Cupboard 'With Pewter and Enamel Panel'. Number 845 and 926, 7s 6d extra.'

Oak hall mirror with copper panel of tulips. R1410

103 Hilliard E. 1993.

104 The Medmenham Pottery was established on Marlow Common in Buckinghamshire in 1898 by Conrad Dressler a sculptor who had been working at the Della Robbia Pottery in Birkenhead. Dressler was financed by William Hudson, the soap magnate until 1906 when the business closed although the tiles continued to be made by J H Barratt & Co in Stoke-on-Trent. The company specialised in small architectural tiles which were combined to create large wall panels. Medmenham Pottery was established with Arts and Crafts principles firmly in mind and emphasis on the use of traditional methods of hand pressing or dust pressing gave the tiles a naive quality. Local materials were used in preference to those brought from outside of the area. C.F.A. Voysey was know to have designed some tiles for this company. Their work was exhibited at the Paris Exhibition 1900 and the 1903 Arts and Crafts Exhibition in London. See also note 75.

105 Liberty and Co. Yuletide Gifts. 1898.

106 I am indebted to Dr Roger Shuff who undertook the research to establish registration for R395643.

107 The Studio 1903 Vol 20 1903 p112.

108 The Furniture Record April17 1903 p421. It is worth noting that other panels have been observed in Shapland and Petter furniture which included 'Robin Hood' Archers 1160, Hall Mirror Pilgrims 1156, Riders with Hounds 2426, Mediaeval lady cabinet 853, Knights in woodland 867.

109 The Art of the Modern School. Harry S Curry. The Artist May/Aug 1901 p205

110 Shapland and Petter High Class Furniture. Decorative Firescreens. R1894a p11.

111 Shapland. H. P. 1926 p17.

112 The Furniture Record. September 15 1899 p146.

113 See detailed description of technique in Shapland. H. P. 1926 p25.

114 Ibid.

115 North Devon Journal October 29 1874 p 5. see also Athenaeum Box 56/106. Documents re School of Art & Science Barnstaple.

116 North Devon Journal December 11, 1879. see also Dec 18.

117 Some art aspects of the 19th century; an essay given to the Barnstaple Reading Circle by Miss Partridge and printed in the North Devon Journal 1st February 1900 p6.

118 North Devon Journal 4th May, 1905 p8, cols. b & c. 'Grand Art & Loan Exhibition at Barnstaple in aid of the North Devon Infirmary'. 'In the modern room was some exquisite local work taking the form of a case of Jewellery and combs designed by Mr F J Partridge, son of Mr James Partridge of Pilton, Barnstaple, with some charming miniature portraits enamelled on silver by Miss M Hart, an Academician. Some of Mr Partridge's exceedingly clever work, which was generally admired, was shown at the St Louis exhibition, where it received most favourable notice. It included gold pendants set with precious stones, hatpins in horn (very novel); comb set with Mexican opals, a silver box engraved with Niello (quite a lost art), combs set with amethysts and moonstones and a gold comb with transparent enamel. Mrs Partridge lent some very fine old Ceylon embroidery and two volumes of the famous Kelmscott press in vellum bind by William Morris with centre panels by Sir Edward Burne-Jones......In a greenwood cabinet lent by Messrs Shapland & Petter was a famous collection of curios belonging to various notables.'

119 The Studio Vol 21 1900 p147.

120 North Devon Journal December 1892.

121 C.R.Ashbee Lectures and Examiners Reports Autumn 1893. In Crawford 1985p 52.

122 The British Architect Dec 20 1901 p439.

123 The Studio vol 27.1904 p212,213.

124 The Studio vol 24 1902.

125 Shapland and Petter Archive. Museum of Barnstaple and North Devon. Indenture Papers. Mr W.H. Rudge.1888.

126 The Cabinet Maker and Complete house furnisher Vol 1 Dec 1880 p88.

127 See Bolitho H 1943 for listings of Batsford publications on furniture and design.

128 Kornwolf 1972 fig 68 p126.

129 Arwas.V1983 p33,34.

130 Liberty and Co. Furniture for Town Flats and Country Houses 1902 p7.

131 Liberty and Co. Book of Furniture Sketches Westminster Archive also Liberty and Co. Furniture for Town Flats and Country Houses 1902 p16.

132 Kornwolf J.D. 1972 gives details of a design for a house for Mr H.A. Cartwright in Barnstaple which was prepared in 1896, by Baillie Scott's practice. HS Morris who was in partnership with Baillie Scott placed both of their signatures on the drawings. Baillie Scott was also believed to have designed house in Sherborne in Dorset and another in Devonshire. p 542.

133 Wylie and Lochhead Catalogue circa 1902.

134 The Furniture Record. Sept 25 1903 p303.

135 CHB Quennell designs Art Workers Quarterly 1889/90 p313. See also Illustration by CHB Quennell for Heal's Catalogue of Plain Oak Furniture; St Ives Suite designed by Ambrose Heal. 1898. NB It is not certain whether the design for the heart pierced splat originated with Ambrose Heal or C.H.B. Quennell as both appeared to use it around this period.

136 Ibid.

137 Shapland H.P. 1909.

138 Shapland H.P. 1926.

139 The Furniture Record. July 26 1901 July 26 p55 and 56. The design for the chimney piece illustrated 6.23 was published in about 1905 but the details of the publication of the drawing are uncertain. A copy exists in the Shapland and Petter archive research files at Barnstaple and North Devon Museum.

140 Rudd.J.H.1912, 1930.

141 North Devon Journal. August 4. 191 .

142 The Studio Yearbook of Decorative Art 1909. The Leading European Designers and Craftsmen p117.

143 There is evidence in the archive ledgers that Shapland and Petter 'bought in' a small amount of furniture, to the value of several hundred pounds in one particular year. No indication of what these items were has been found.

144 The history of the Raleigh family in Devon shows that they came over with William the Conqueror a thousand years ago and settled at that time in the manor of Raleigh in Pilton near Barnstaple The hamlet of Raleigh, down the hill from the mansion, was the place where water-powered mills operated off the River Yeo from very early times until the mid 20th century. The mill race and old sluices etc. are still on site, and the sound of rushing water is still to be heard there. Sir Walter Raleigh, as the most well remembered member of the family in modern times, was chosen as an emblem for the firm of Shapland & Petter and it was for this reason that the name continued after they left the old mill and moved to their new site for in Barnstaple and better access to rail, road and water links. J. L. Vivian, The Visitations of Devon (Exeter, 1895) pp.638/9 pedigree of the Raleigh family. I am indebted to Margaret Reed for this information.

145 White J.P. 1901.

Bibliography

Agius. Pauline. British Furniture 1880-1915(London 1978)

Arwas.V. Liberty Style (London. 1983)

Aslin, Elizabeth Nineteenth –Century furniture (London 1962)

Anscombe. Isabelle. Arts and Crafts Style (Oxford 1991)

Anscombe. Isabelle and Gere Charlotte Arts and Crafts in Britain (London, 1978)

Ashbee.C.R. Craftsmanship In Competitive Industry. London. Nd

Baillie Scott. M.H Houses and Gardens. (Woodbridge 1995)

Bolitho. H A Batsford Century, (London 1943)

Burkhauser. Jude (ed) 'Glasgow Girls' Women in Art and Design 1880 - 1920 (Glasgow School of Art exhib catalogue. 1990)

Calloway. S. The House of Liberty Masters of Style and Decoration London 1992

Carruthers. Annette and Greensted. Mary Good Citizens Furniture The Arts and Crafts Collections at Cheltenham. (London 1994)

Carruthers. Annette and Greensted. Arts and Crafts Living Objects from the Cheltenham Collections (Cheltenham and London 1994)

Clarke. E.E. A Handbook of Plant form for students of design. (London 1905)

Cooper. Jeremy. Victorian and Edwardian Furniture and Interiors; From the Gothic Revival to Art Nouveau (London 1987)

Crane. W Of the Revival of Design and Handicraft in Arts and Crafts Essays, p12

Crawford. Alan. C.R.Ashbee; Architect, Designer and Romantic Socialist (Newhaven and London 1985)

Crawford. Alan(ed) By Hammer and Hand, The Arts and Crafts Movement in Birmingham. (Birmingham Museums and Art Gallery. Exhib cat. 1994)

Cumming. Elizabeth and Kaplan, Wendy. The Arts and Crafts Movement (London 1991)

Davey Peter. Arts and Crafts Architecture (London 1980)

Davidson. H. C. The Book of the Home (London 1904)

Day L.F. Lettering in Ornament (London 1902)

Day L.F. Nature as Ornament (London 1908)

Day L.F. Alphabets Old and New (London 1898)

Dwight. W. The Century Dictionary. The Times (London New York `1899) Eastlake.C.L. Hints on Household Taste (London 1872)

Edgeler. A. Art Potteries of Barnstaple (Hants 1990)

Edwards. C. Victorian Furniture Technology and Design (Manchester 1993)

Forty. A. Objects of Desire Design and Society 1780 to 1950 (London1986)

Ellwood. G.M. English Furniture and Decoration (London 1909)

Ellwood. GM. Designs of in Trade Catalogue of Bath Cabinet Makers. Unknown date, NAL

Gameson. R. The study of the Bayeux Tapestry (Woodbridge 1997)

Greensted, Mary. Gimson and the Barnsleys Wonderful Furniture of a

Commonplace Kind (Stroud 1980)

Greensted. Mary The Arts and Crafts Movement in the Cotswolds (Stroud 1992)

Harvey. C. and Press. J. William Morris Design and Enterprise in Victorian Britain (Manchester 1991)

Heal and Sons. Catalogue of Plain Oak Furniture (London. 1898)

Helland. J. The Studios of Frances and Margaret and Macdonald (Manchester 1996)

Hilliard. E. Fired Earth Decorating With Tiles (Melrose BG 1993)

Hitchmough. Wendy. C.F.A. Voysey (London 1995)

Hitchmough. Wendy. The Arts and Crafts Home (London 2000)

Lethaby. W.R. Architecture; Mysticism and Myth (London 1891)

Kornwolf,. James D. MH Baillie Scott and the Arts and Crafts Movement; Pioneers of

Modern Design (Baltimore and London 1972).

Morris. W. Art and Socialism (London1948) p 653.

Liberty's 1875-1975 (Victoria and Albert Museum, London exhib cat 1975)

Liberty Archives. Westminster Archives. Westminster Council. London

Lister Sutcliffe. G. The Modern Carpenter, Joiner and Cabinet-Maker. (London 1905)

Livingstone K.Parry L. eds. International Arts and Crafts exhib cat. (London 2005)

McCarthy. Fiona The Simple Life C.R. Ashbee in the Cotswolds (London 1981)

McCarthy. Fiona William Morris: A Life for our Time (London 1994)

Muthesius. H. Das Englische Haus (Berlin1904-5;Abridged English translation of 2nd ed. D Sharpe London 1979)

Norman and Stacey Ltd. Catalogue of Artistic Furniture, decorations carpets and antiques (London 1910)

Parry. Linda Textiles of the Arts and Crafts Movement (London 1988)

Pevsner. N. Pioneers of the Modern Movement from William Morris to Walter Gropius (London 1936).

Reed. M 2004. Shapland and Petter of Barnstaple Celebrating 150 years (Barnstaple 2004)

Rudd. J.H. Practical cabinet making and draughting (London 1912)

Rudd. J.H Manual training in relation to handicraft, for teachers in manual training centres, junior technical, senior and central schools. (London 1930)

Shapland.H.P. Style Schemes in Antique Furnishing. Interiors and their treatment (London 1909)

Shapland. H.P. The Practical Decoration of Furniture (London 1926)

Strong.H.W. Industries of North Devon (Barnstaple1889)

Timms and Webb 35 Styles of English Furniture (London 1904)

Tinniswood.A The Arts and Crafts House (London 1999)

Vivian.J.L The Visitations of Devon (Exeter 1895)

Whiteway. M and Gere. C Nineteenth-Century Design from Pugin to Mackintosh (London 1993)

White. JP Catalogue of Furniture made at the Pygtle Works Bedford by John. P. White, designed by M.H. Baillie Scott. 1901

William. R. Dream Worlds. Consumerism in Nineteenth Century France (London 1998)

Wilson. A.N. The Victorians (London 2002)

Wylie and Lochhead, Wylie and Lochhead artistic house furnishers (Glasgow Circa 1902)

Periodicals

Journal of the Furniture History Society.

The Art Journal (London 1839-1912)

The Artist (London 1880-1902)

The Cabinet Maker and Art Furnisher (London 1880 to 1902)

The Cabinet Maker and Complete house furnisher (London 1902 1961)

Art Workers Quarterly (London 1902-6)

The British Architect (London 1886-1919)

The Builder (London 1842-1966)

Furniture and Decoration (London 1893-99)

The Furniture Gazette (London 1873-93)

The Furniture Record (London 1899-1962)

The Studio (London 1893-)

The Art Decorator (London 1890 to 1914)

North Devon Journal

Source of Images

Museum of Barnstaple and North Devon. 2.2, 2.4 2.5, 2.9, 2.10,

Small photos and 'ghosted' images; High Class Furniture and Catalogue of Drawings respectively.

Authors collection 1.6, 2.6, 2.7, 3.1, 3.2, 3.13, 3.14, 3,15, 3.20,

Mr Adam Brawn Meek. 3.24

Mr Vincent Duffy 4.21

V&A Images. 1.1, 1.2, 1.11 1.13, 1.16, 2.3, 3.7 to 3.11, 3.19, 3.23, 3.25 to 3.28, 4.23, 5.15, 5.22, 5.23, 6.21, 6.23, 7.5,

National Archives, Registration of Designs. 3.29.

Hillhouse Antiques and Decorative Arts. 4.2,

Art Furniture. 5.49,

William Morris Gallery. 1.7

Chetlenham Museum and Art Gallery 1.8, 6.10

The Studio images collection Mr Paul Gilby, Philip Bowditch

Collection P Gilby. 1.14, 4.26,

West Yorkshire Archive Service 3.3, 4.28 small picture,

Subject Index

About the Author

Daryl Bennett is a medical sociologist working independently for government and public sector agencies to help develop treatment for people with drug dependency.

As a hobby he has developed an interest in the Arts and Crafts movement and in 2002 he set up a website artscrafts.org.uk as an educational resource. During 2004/5 he worked as the voluntary project manager for the Heritage Lottery Project in Barnstaple. He lives in Sheffield with his partner and two children.